AF646336

COOPERATIVE AUDITING

COOPERATIVE AUDITING

By

Dr. M.Karthikeyan

Assistant Professor

Department of Cooperatives

Institute of Cooperatives & Development Studies

Ambo University

P.B. No. 511

Ambo, West Shoa

Ethiopia

DISCOVERY PUBLISHING HOUSE PVT. LTD.

NEW DELHI-110 002

Published by:

Tilak Wasan

DISCOVERY PUBLISHING HOUSE PVT. LTD.

4383/4A, Ansari Road, Darya Ganj

New Delhi-110 002 (India)

Phone : +91-11-23279245, 43596064-65

Fax : +91-11-23253475

E-mail : parul.wasan@gmail.com
discoverypublishinghouse@gmail.com

web : www.discoverypublishinggroup.com

First Edition: **2012**

ISBN: 978-93-5056-001-3

Cooperative Auditing

© 2012, **Author**

All rights reserved. No part of this publication should be reproduced, stored in a retrieval system, or transmitted in any form or by any means: electronic, mechanical, photocopying, recording or otherwise, without the prior written permission of the author and the publisher.

This book has been published in good faith that the material provided by authors is original. Every effort is made to ensure accuracy of material, but the publisher and printer will not be held responsible for any inadvertent error(s). In case of any dispute, all legal matters are to be settled under Delhi jurisdiction only.

Printed at:
Shree Balaji Art Press
Delhi

Preface

Dear learners! It is my pleasure to introduce the text book on "Cooperative Auditing' to you. It has been designed into two parts in a detailed manner so as to help you understand the application of auditing principles in the cooperative sector. Cooperative Auditing is somewhat different from other courses. I think you may have studied cooperative accounting course. The cooperative accounting process ends with auditing. The last stage of cooperative accounting is cooperative auditing; without which the accounts maintained by the cooperatives are not legally recognized. Only after the audit is over and audit report is submitted along with the audit certificate, the accounts maintained by the cooperatives are legally accepted and approved. So, dear learners, audit has got its own value and it is a very important one, which is to be done regularly every year by the cooperatives as per the cooperative law or proclamation.

This work is based on my experience as teacher, trainer and researcher in the field of information systems, management and cooperatives for more than 15 years. The present work is based on Under Graduate programme and outcome of my teaching and research experience, articles published in reputed journals, and discussions with cooperative officials and auditors. This book will be very much useful to the student of under graduate, and also to accounting and auditing professionals and managers in companies, and the trainers who are working in various training establishments. I have drawn the inputs from various materials; papers, journals, books and I have consulted several of my friends, colleagues and field experts. I am ever grateful and thankful to them for their immense support and healthy criticism. I hope that the readers of this book will get knowledge on Cooperative Auditing. Any useful comments, suggestions to improve the present version are welcome and solicited from the readers. I am thankful and grateful to Parul Wasan, Discovery Publishing House Pvt. Ltd., New Delhi for publishing this book neatly under his renowned label for the accounting knowledge community.

M.KARTHIKEYAN

Contents

Part — I

General Principles of Audit

1 Auditing
An Overview

History of Audit

The necessary and justification of audit has been felt after evolution of a system of accounts to record the transactions of an organization. It was felt that an independent examination of the accounts was necessary to ensure their accuracy and to act as a deterrent to willful manipulation. Audit therefore, is a system to check upon persons, whose business it was to record the receipt and disbursement of money on behalf of others. Audit has come to assume its present day characteristics, consequent on the industrial revolution in Europe due to the formation of numerous joint stock companies and other corporate undertakings with large sums of capital contributed by individuals under the management of a set of few individuals. It was found necessary to subject these transactions to an independent examination and security in order to satisfy the shareholders that their investment was safe. In Ethiopia it has been practiced for very many years in the government offices, companies and cooperatives.

Meaning and Definition of Audit

The term 'Audit' is derived from the Latin word 'audire' which means, 'to hear'. The literal meaning of audit is to hear and the auditor is the person who hears the explanations from the persons accountable for keeping accounts. Thus, audit or auditing means that an act of checking or examining the truth of accounts of an enterprise. The purpose, aim and objective of audit may vary depending on the type of business and ownership position of an organization.

Definition of Audit

Here are some definitions given by different authors.

Audit is an examination of accounts of business concern with a view to ascertain the true state of its affairs. In the words of Dicker *"an audit is the examination of the accounts of a business and certifying their accuracy"*.

Auditing is instituted with a view to find out of correctness of recorded accounts. Entries made in the books of account are verified with the original documents evidencing the transaction. The verification is done in such a way as to ascertain obvious that if the verification is to be impartial and fruit bearing, it should be done by a person who is neither concerned with the maintenance of accounts nor with the conduct of affairs of the business.

L.R. Dicksee defines, "an audit is an examination of accounting records undertaken with a view to establishing whether they correctly and completely reflect the transactions to which they purport to relate."

According to A.W. Hanson, "An audit is an examination of such records to establish their reliability and the reliability of statements drawn from them".

Auditing may, thus be defined as a thorough and critical examination of accounts of any institution with the original documents relating thereto by and independent agency in such a manner as to ascertain if they exhibit a true and correct view of the state of its affairs. In short, audit is an independent security of accounts with a view to find out their correctness. The essential requisite of audit is that the person employed for it should be independent of those concerned with the conduct of business and maintenance of accounts.

The Nature and Scope of Audit

The scope and nature of an audit is dependent on the terms of agreement between the auditor and client and on statutory requirements and the requirements of the relevant professional bodies.

- A properly conducted audit is organized to cover adequately all aspects of the organization as far as they are relevant to the financial statements subject to examination.
- The auditor has to ensure that information contained in the underlying accounting data and other source data is reliable and sufficient as the basis for the preparation of the financial statements.
- The responsibility is heavy and cannot be discharged without a full realization of the professional skill and judgment, which need to be exercised in carrying out his duties.

Essential Characteristics of Auditing

The following are the essential characteristics of auditing:

- Audit is an independent, scientific and critical examination of books of accounts or records of a business;
- Such examination enables the auditor to satisfy himself that the balance sheet and the profit and loss account are properly drawn up;
- Detection of errors and frauds is an integral part of auditing;
- Audit job is performed by an independent person or body of persons qualified for the job;
- Vouching and routine checking of documents and verification and valuation of assets and liabilities are done; and
- Auditor may satisfy himself about the correctness, accuracy and authenticity of records and accounts and submit his report accordingly.

Auditing is a very responsible task. It is extensive ad onerous; it constitutes different phases of work. To begin with, extensive vouching is done. The entries made in the books of original entry are verified with all available documentary evidence in order to see if they are in order , genuine and constitutional. Besides verification tactful enquiries are made to ensue that the books of accounts themselves are correct and reflect nothing but truth.

After the vouching is over the ledger postings are verified find the arithmetical accuracy of the accounts is tested by the agreement of the trial balance or the statement of receipts and disbursements, as the case may be.

The next phase of work is the verification of final account and balance sheet. The latter is closely scrutinized in order to ascertain whether it exhibits the true financial position of the business as on the date. Its examination is finalized by verifying the existence of assets and checking their valuation.

Finally, the correctness of balance sheet and final account is certified and the result of auditing are reported to the concerned authorities with all significant facts in unequivocal terms.

The scope of auditing is extensive and dynamic as well in the early stages; there was merely a cash audit. That is, only transactions connected with receipts and disbursements of cash were verified. Staring from that crude form of examination, audit has gradually developed in to a verification of transactions of all possible nature inherent in modern business time passes ad we with time industries and commerce are rapidly developing and the practice of auditing is also growing up to cope up with such development.

The main Objects of Audit

The object (or purpose) of auditing is threefold:

- In the first place, it aims at ascertaining the exact financial position of the business as on a particular date.

- In the second place, it aims at detecting errors and frauds.
- Lastly, it aims at preventing occurrence and recurrence of errors and frauds in future by means of its moral effects.

The first two are primary objects and the last object is corollary to the primary ones.

The Ascertainment of Financial Position

The exact financial position of a business on a date is revealed by the balance sheet as on that date. Balance sheet is a statement of assets and liabilities and other remaining balances. It shows how the capital stands invested in different assets. It discloses whether the balance sheet has been drawn up in conformity wit the books of account, which are correct by themselves. A correct balance sheet will show the actual state of affairs of the business. The presentation of a correct balance sheet ultimately depends on the detection of errors and frauds and their rectification.

The Detection of Errors

Errors are committed intentionally and unintentionally as well. Unintentional errors may or may not have adverse effects. But intentional errors might amount to fraudulent manipulation of accounts, and result in considerable loss to the business. The auditors should therefore, trace out the cause of any error however slight it might appear to be. There are four main classes of errors, viz.:

1. error of omission;
2. error of commission;
3. error of principle; and
4. compensating error.

1. *Error of omission* — It arises when any transaction is omitted to be recorded in a book of original entry e.g., an item of credit purchase omitted to be entered in the

purchases daybook. This kind of omission will not affect the agreement of he trial balance in as much as it affects two opposite account to an equal extent. Hence the difficulty of its detection. It can, however, be detected by comparing the original documents like receipts, invoices, vouchers, bills, etc., and by examining the statement of account and confirmation memos received from parties. An error of omission is rectified by passing an appropriate entry in the concerned book for the transaction which has been omitted.

2. *Error of commission* — it arises out of incorrect or omission of postings, and of mistakes in castings and carrying forwards. It might also occur when a transaction is wrongly entered in the book of original entry: e.g., an item of credit sales for $.515 wrongly recorded in the sales daybook as $.550.

It is also known as clerical error. The following are common instances of errors of commission:

(i) Omission of posting of an account from the book of original entry to the ledger — e.g., salaries A/c omitted to be posted in to the ledger. His kind of error will be revealed by the difference in trial balance because it is one sided.

(ii) Wrong posting of an item to the debit of an account instead of to its credit or vice versa — e.g., an item of $.350 received from 'A' on account wrongly posted under the debit side of A's A/c. it will affect the agreement of the trial balance to the extent of double the amount of the item.

(iii) Posting of wrong amounts to correct heads of accounts — e.g., a sum of $.46.50 paid for wages wrongly posted to the wages A/c as $.46.15. This error will also causes a difference in trial balance.

(iv) Posting an item to a wrong account of the same class — e.g., an item of payment made on Asfaw's

A/c wrongly posted to Asfaw & Son's A/c. Errors of this type will be discovered when any notice is received from the parties objecting to the balances shown against them in the statements of account sent to them.

(v) Mistakes in striking our the balances of ledger accounts — these would be revealed by the corresponding differences in trial balance.

(vi) Mistakes in castings and carrying —forwards — these errors will also affect the agreement of the trial balance.

In general, errors of commission can be detected by mere routine checking, i.e., checking of postings, calculations on castings. They are rectified by carrying out necessary adjustments in the concerned accounts or by passing rectification entries as the case may be.

3. *Error of principle* — it arises on account of a transaction being recorded in a fundamentally in correct manner through lack of knowledge of the principles of accountancy. It arises when a revenue item is wrongly posted to another class of revenue account. For example an item of wages paid for labourers might be wrongly posted to 'trade charges'. It is also caused by treating the revenue item as a capital one or vice versa. Incorrect allocation of expenditure between capital and revenue, inadequate provisos for depreciation, bad debt, etc., are other instances of error of principle.

Error of principle is not disclosed by mere routing checking intelligent enquiry and research should be made and the auditor should take the utmost care to detect them, since they vitally affect the correctness of final account and balance sheet.

4. *Compensating error* — it is an error of dangerous type. It arises out of one error or a series of errors being

counterbalanced by another error or series of errors. It does not affect the agreement of he trial balance. It might or might not affect the profit or loss. If the original error and the compensating error both occur in a revenue account, the profit and loss account will not be affected. But if one arises in a revenue account and the other in a capital account the profit and loss account as well as the balance sheet will be affected. Compensating errors will be detected by careful verification of postings, castings and carrying—forwards, and by intelligent investigation of ledger accounts.

The Detection of Frauds

The detection of frauds is by far the most important part of an auditor's duties and it is also the main purpose of his appointment in most of the cases. Frauds are of two kinds:

(i) Misappropriation or defalcation of cash or goods; and

(ii) Falsification or manipulation of accounts not resulting in actual deflection.

(i) *Misappropriation of cash or goods* — when cash is misappropriated, it is contrived to conceal the misappropriation by including fictitious payments and by omitting receipts. The form can be detected by careful examination of vouchers; bills wage sheets and other original documentary evidences in support of payments. The latter is discovered by checking the debit side of the cashbook with original document such as cash diaries, counterfoils of receipts, etc. If cash received from debtors is misappropriated, it can be revealed by the examination of statements of accounts received from them as regards the misappropriation of goods, it is but impossible to detect the fraud unless accurate stock records are kept there should prevail some definite system of internal check in respect of the incomings and outgoings of goods.

(ii) *Fraudulent manipulation of accounts* — falsification of accounts not involving misappropriation is often perpetrated by men in positions of trust and responsibility like directors or managers itch the object of bolstering up the concern by showing fictitious profits in order to pay large dividends or to obtain large loans, etc. The auditors should therefore, be vigilant and should not be carried away by the false information and explanations given to him considerable searching enquires should be made to discover such frauds.

The extent and the amount of detailed checking and scrutiny that have to be made by the auditors for discovering error and frauds depend on the circumstances of each cash and the efficient operation of internal check, if any, in vogue.

The Prevention of Errors and Frauds

Apart from its concrete functions an efficient audit is also having a moral effect. The very fact that an auditor is going to check the accounts will, by itself, act as a moral check up on parties concerned. A systematic and regular audit creates a sense of responsibility and fear in the minds of employees of a concern and they are forced to act as far as possible honestly without committing errors and frauds, as these will be ultimately exposed in the course of Audit. In this sense, Audit is said to be aiming at preventing occurrence and recurrence of errors and frauds in future.

The Advantages of Audit

The significant magnitude of the utility of an efficient Audit can be inferred from the fact that even business concerns, which have no legal obligation to subject their accounts to audit, volunteer to get their accounts audited periodically. Indeed, Audit is a utility service and the advantages derived from it are many and varied. The common advantages accruing from Audit in general may be enumerated as follows:

- The detection and prevention of errors and frauds is an advantage common to all classes of Audit.
- The ascertainment of the true and correct view of the state of affairs of a concern helps its proprietors to find out whether their business is sound or not.
- The publication of a Balance sheet with the certificate of a reputed Auditors gives a better status to the business and thereby helps to command the confidence of the public.
- Financial help from Banks and other Institutions will be easily coming forth to those concerns whose accounts are subjected to Audit.
- Audit is the best. Means to ascertain how for a concern has been able to carry on its business to achieve the purpose for which it was created.
- Audit also helps to create a sense of regularity and responsibility in the employees of the business and stimulates the efficiency of their work.
- A regular Audit will also disclose the weak points either in the conduct of the affairs of business or in maintaining the accounts, the elimination of which will help to improve the business.
- Audited accounts are more relied on for the purposes of levy of Sales Tax, Income Tax, etc. and help to avoid the possibilities of over — assessments and consequent litigations.
- In the case of undertakings jointly owned by two or more persons, they rely on audited accounts for the correctness of the net profits to be divided among themselves.
- The sale of a business as a going concern is considerably facilitated, if proper accounts are maintained and audited.
- Where the affairs of a business are not personally conducted by all the proprietors but by a small group of them on behalf of all, Audit will act as a check up on that executive body.

- Audit also acts as a safeguard against frauds and manipulation of accounts.
- Lastly efficient Audit safeguards the interest of the creditors of a concern.

In short, Audit is indispensable for all kinds of undertaking, and a business without Audit is considered to be next to nothing.

The Distinction Between Accountancy and Audit

You might have studied accountancy course. Now you know the meaning and basics of auditing.

Audit is entirely different from Accountancy. While Accountancy is a Science as well as an Art of recording business transactions under appropriate heads of accounts in a set of books, Auditing in a Science of examination of accounts with a view to find out their accuracy.

Accountancy comprises recording of transactions, agreement of the Trial Balance and the preparation of Final Account and Balance Sheet. Audit is quite distinct from this function. It does not entail recording of transactions, or preparation of Final Accounts. It involves an examination of the Balance Sheet and Profit and Loss Account (prepared by others) together with books, accounts and documentary evidences in order to ascertain their correctness.

The object of Account-keeping is to record the financial effect of all transactions of a given period with a view to find out their net result and the financial condition of the business as well. On the other hand, the object of Audit is to detect and prevent errors and frauds and to find out if the Balance sheet reflects the real state of affairs of the undertaking. The person who is engaged for maintaining the accounts cannot, therefore, be called an Auditor, even if he is a professional Auditor. Only the person who is entrusted with the task of examination of accounts prepared by others will be called an Auditor.

Thus, Accountancy and Auditing are two different Sciences though they are complementary to one another. But between these two functions it is generally thought that if a professional auditor prepares account, he necessarily guarantees their accuracy. This is evidently a wrong idea if he is engaged for preparing accounts; he is acting only as an accountant and not in any way as an auditor. The duty of an auditor is to check and report up on the completed work of others.

Self-learning Activity

Try to answer the following questions on your own:

1. Define Audit.
2. Discuss the nature and scope of audit.
3. What are the objectives of audit?
4. Explain the error of commission?
5. What is error of principle?
6. Discuss about misappropriation of cash or goods?
7. What are the advantages of audit?

Summary

- Audit is an examination of accounts of business concern with a view to ascertain the true state of its affairs.
- The scope and nature of an audit is dependent on the terms of agreement between the auditor and client and on statutory requirements and the requirements of the relevant professional bodies. The scope of auditing is extensive and dynamic as well.
- Objectives of audit is three-fold — ascertaining the exact financial position of the business as on a particular date; detecting errors and frauds; and preventing occurrence and recurrence of errors and frauds in future by means of its moral effects.

- Audit is indispensable for all kinds of undertaking, and a business without Audit is considered to be next to nothing.
- Thus, Accountancy and Auditing are two different Sciences though they are complementary to one another.

2 Generally Accepted Auditing Standards

Auditing Standards

Auditing Standards are guidelines to aid auditors in fulfilling their professional responsibilities in the audit of historical financial statements. They include consideration of professional qualities such as competence and independence, reporting requirements, and evidence.

The broadest guidelines available are the ten generally accepted auditing standards (GAAS). Developed by the American Institute of Charted Public Accountants (AICPA) in 1947, they have, with minimal changes, remained the same. These standards are not sufficiently specific to provide any meaningful guide to practitioners, but they do represent a framework upon which the AICPA can provide interpretations. These ten standards, summarized hereunder, are stated in their entirety as follows:

General Standards

1. The examination is to be performed by a person or persons having adequate technical training and proficiency as an auditor.
2. In all matters relating to the assignment, independence in mental attitude is to be maintained by the auditor or auditors.
3. Due professional care is to be exercised in the performance of the examination and the preparation of the report.

Standards of Field Work

1. The work is to be adequately planned and assistants, if any, are to be properly supervised.
2. The auditor should obtain a sufficient understanding of the internal control structure to plan the audit and to determine the nature, timing, and extent of tests to be performed.
3. Sufficient competent evidential matter is to be obtained through inspection, observation, inquiries, and confirmations to afford a reasonable basis for an opinion regarding the financial statements under examination.

Standards of Reporting

1. The report shall state whether the financial statements are presented in accordance with generally accepted accounting principles.
2. The report shall identify those circumstances, which such principles have not been consistently observed in the current period in relation to the preceding period.
3. Informative disclosures in the financial statements are to be regarded as reasonably adequate unless otherwise stated in the report.
4. The report shall either contain an expression of opinion regarding the financial statements, taken as a whole, or an assertion to the effect that an opinion cannot be expressed. When an overall opinion cannot be expressed, the reasons therefore should be stated. In all cases where an auditor's name is associated with financial statements, the report should contain a clear-cut indication of the character of the auditor's examination, if any, and the degree of responsibility he is taking.

Statements on Auditing Standards (SASs)

The Statements on Auditing Standards (SASs) are the most authoritative references available to auditors. These statements are issued by the AICPA and are interpretations of generally accepted auditing standards. All SASs are given two classification numbers: an SAS and an AU number. For example, the Statement on Auditing Standards: The relationship of generally accepted auditing standards to quality control standards is SAS 25 and AU 161. The SAS number identifies the order in which it was issued in relation to other SASs; the AU number identifies its location in the AICPA codification of all SASs.

Generally accepted auditing standards and statements on auditing standards are regarded as authoritative literature because every member of the profession is required to follow their recommendations whenever they are applicable. Here is the study of the standards and frequent reference to the SASs.

Adequate technical training and proficiency: The first standard is normally interpreted as requiring the auditor to have formal education in auditing, accounting, adequate practical experience for the work being performed, and continuing professional education.

Independence in mental attitude: The code of professional ethics and the SASs stress the need for independence.

Due professional care: The interpretation is that the auditor is a professional responsible for fulfilling his or her duties diligently and carefully.

Adequate planning and supervision: The first standard of field work standards deals with ascertaining that the engagement is sufficiently well planned to ensure an adequate audit and proper supervision of assistants.

Understand the internal control structure: The client's internal control is one of the most widely accepted concepts in the theory and practice of auditing.

Sufficient competent evidence: The decision as to how much evidence to accumulate for a given set of circumstances is one requiring professional judgment.

Four reporting standards: The four reporting standards require the auditor to prepare a report on the financial statements taken as a whole, including informative disclosures.

Self-learning Activity

Try to answer the following questions on your own:

1. Write about the generally accepted auditing standards.
2. Write short notes on: Statements on Auditing Standards.

Summary

- There are ten generally accepted audit standards under three categories: general, field work and reporting; and related statements on audit standards.

3 Professional Ethics and Legal Liabilities of Auditors

Professional Ethics

The underlying reason for a code of ethics for any profession is the need for public confidence in the quality of service by the profession, regardless of the individual providing it. The code of professional ethics has a significant effect on what auditors do. It is also a significant influence on practitioners. The introduction to the AICPA Code of Professional Ethics include a quotation from Marcus Aurelius that effectively summarizes what should be expected from a professional: "A man should be upright, not kept upright".

A code of ethics can consists of general statements of ideal conduct or specific rules that define unacceptable behaviour. The advantage of the general statements is the emphasis on positive activities that encourage a high level of performance. The disadvantage is the difficulty of enforcing general ideals, because there are no minimum standards of behaviour.

The AICPA code of professional ethics has attempted to accomplish both the objectives of general statements of ideal conduct and of specific rules. There are four parts to the code: concepts, rules of conduct, interpretations, and ethical rulings. The guidelines are listed in order of increasing specificity; the concepts provide ideal standards of conduct, whereas ethical rulings are highly specific. The four parts are summarized in the following exhibit.

Exhibit — Code of Professional Ethics

Concepts	— Ideal standards of ethical conduct stated in philosophical terms. They are not enforceable.
Rules of conduct	— Minimum standards of ethical conduct stated as specific rules. They are enforceable.
Interpretations	— Interpretations of the rules of conduct by the AICPA division of professional ethics. They are not enforceable, but a practitioner must justify departure.
Ethical rulings	— Published explanations and answers to questions about the rules of conduct submitted to the AICPA by practitioners and others interested in ethical requirements. They are not enforceable, but a practitioner must justify departure.

Concepts of Professional Ethics: It includes five ethical principles. They are listed hereunder:

1. Independence, integrity and objectivity;
2. Competence and technical standards;
3. Responsibilities to clients;
4. Responsibilities to colleagues; and
5. Other responsibilities and practices.

Rule of Conduct: It says about the level of conduct of the practitioners. As in any profession, the level varies among practitioners. Some operate at high level, whereas others operate as close to the minimum level as possible. Unfortunately, some also conduct themselves below the minimum level set by the profession.

Interpretation of Rules of Conduct: The division of professional ethics prepares each interpretation based on a consensus of a committee made up principally of public accounting practitioners. Interpretations are not enforceable, but a departure from the interpretations would be difficult for a practitioner to justify in a disciplinary hearings.

Ethical Rulings: Rulings are explanations by the executive committee of the professional ethics division of specific factual circumstances.

Legal Liabilities of Auditors

Professionals have always had a duty to provide a reasonable level of care while performing work for those they serve. This responsibility is an implied part of the contract entered into between any professional and his or her client.

Under common law, the duty of due care is owned to third-party non-clients only in limited circumstances: those in which the third party is a known and intended beneficiary of the professional work. In recent years, the courts have frequently interpreted common law to broaden the availability of legal remedies to parties other than clients and the narrow, 'known beneficiary' group. In addition, the courts have interpreted the federal securities law broadly to create additional liabilities. There are no simple reasons for this trend, but there are major factors:

The factors are:

- The growing awareness of the responsibilities of public accountants by users of financial statements;
- An increased consciousness on the part of the securities and exchange commission (SEC) regarding its responsibility for protecting investors' interests;
- The greater complexity of auditing and accounting due to such factors as the increasing size of business, the existence of the computer, and the intricacies of business operations;
- The deep-pocket concept of liability;
- Willingness to settle legal problems.

Legal Concepts Affecting Liability

There is liability for public accounting work, including auditing, taxes, management advisory services, and accounting and bookkeeping services. The areas of liability in auditing can be classified as:

1. liability to clients;
2. civil liability to third parties under common and statutory law; and
3. Federal securities law.

The several legal concepts apply to all types of lawsuits are the prudent man concept, liability for the acts of others, and the lack of privileged communication.

Liability to Clients

The most common source of liability has been to clients for failure to perform their auditing functions with due care. These law suits often involve defalcations that the auditor has failed to uncover. The client claims that the certified public accountant would have uncovered these if he or she had not been negligent. The lawsuit can be for breach of contract, or it can be a tort action for negligence. Most law suits involving clients are tort rather than breach of contract actions because the amount recoverable under torts is normally larger. In the auditing environment, failure to meet generally accepted auditing standards is often conclusive evidence of negligence.

Auditor's defenses – clients suits: The certified public accountant (CPA) firm normally uses one or a combination of three defenses when there are legal claims by clients: *lack of duty* to perform the service — means that the CPA firm claims there was no implied or expressed contract; *non-negligent performance* in an audit — means that the CPA firm claims that the audit was performed in accordance with generally accepted auditing standards; and *contributory negligence* — means that the CPA firm claims that if the client had performed certain obligations, the loss would not have occurred.

Liability to Third Parties under Common Law

A Charted Public Accountants (CPA) firm may be liable to third parties if a loss was incurred by the claimant due to reliance on misleading financial statements. Third parties include actual and potential stockholders, vendors, bankers and other creditors, employees, and customers.

Auditor's defenses – Third Parties: There are two primary defenses available to auditors in suits by third parties: *non-negligent performance* — if the auditor conducted the audit in accordance with GAAS; and *lack of privities of contract* — depends heavily on the judicial jurisdiction.

Civil Liability under the Federal Securities Law

Although there has been some growth in actions brought against accountants and auditors by their clients or third parties under common law, the greatest growth in Charted Public Accountants (CPA) liability litigation has been under the Federal Securities Laws.

The emphasis on federal remedies has resulted primarily from the recently expanded availability of class-action litigation and the relative ease of obtaining massive recovery from defendants. In addition, several sections of the securities laws impose rather strict liability standards on CPAs. Federal courts are often likely to favour plaintiffs in lawsuits in which there are strict standards.

Self-learning Activity

Try to answer the following questions on your own:

1. What professional ethic the auditors should follow?
2. Write short notes on:
   (*a*) Auditor's legal liability to clients;
   (*b*) legal liability to third parties.

Summary

- There are ten generally accepted audit standards and related statements on audit standards.
- The auditors should follow the professional ethics stated and they have legal liabilities to clients, to third parties under common law, and civil liability under the federal securities laws.

4 Audit Evidence

Audit Evidence Decisions

A major decision facing every auditor is determining the appropriate amount of evidence to accumulate in order to be satisfied that the components of the client's financial statements and the overall statements are fairly stated. This judgment is important because of the prohibitive cost of examining and evaluating all available evidence.

The auditor's decisions on evidence accumulation can be broken into the following four:

1. Which audit procedure to use?
2. Which sample size to select for a given procedure?
3. Which particular items to select from the population?
4. When to perform the procedures?

Audit procedures: These are the detailed instructions for the collection of a particular type of audit evidence that is to be obtained at some time during the audit. In designing audit procedures, it is common to spell them out in sufficiently terms to permit their use as instructions during the audit.

Sample size: Once an audit procedure is selected, it is possible to vary the sample size from one to all the items in the population being tested. The sample size for any given procedure is likely to vary from audit to audit.

Items to select: After the sample size has been determined for a particular audit procedure, it is still necessary to decide the particular items to examine.

Timing: The timing of audit procedures can vary from early in the accounting period to long after it has ended.

Audit Programme: The detailed description of the results of the four evidence decisions for a specific audit is called as audit programme. It always includes a list of the audit procedures. It usually also states the sample size, particular items to select, and the timing of the tests. Normally there is an audit programme section for each component of the audit. The right side of the audit programme includes the audit objectives for each procedure.

Types of Audit Evidence

In deciding which audit procedure to use, there are seven broad category of evidence from which the auditor can choose. These categories, referred to as types of audit evidence.

The various types of audit evidence are listed and discussed hereunder:

- Physical examination
- Confirmation
- Documentation
- Observation
- Inquiries of the client
- Mechanical accuracy
- Analytical procedures

Physical examination: Physical examination is the inspection or count by the auditor of a tangible asset. This type of evidence is most often associated with inventory and cash, but it is also applicable to the verification of securities, notes receivable, and tangible fixed assets. It is one of the most reliable and useful types of audit evidence.

Confirmation: Confirmation describes the receipt of a written response from an independent third party verifying the accuracy of information that was requested by the auditor. Since confirmations come from sources independent of the client, they are a highly regarded and often used type of evidence.

Documentation: Documentation, commonly referred to as vouching, is the auditor's examination of the client's documents and records to substantiate the information that is or should be included in the financial statements. Documents can be conveniently classified as internal and external. An internal document is one that has been prepared and used within the client's organization and is retained without ever going to an outside party such as customer or a vendor. An external document is one that has been in the hands of someone outside the client's organization. The external documents are regarded as more reliable evidence than internal ones.

Observation: Observation is the use of the senses to assess certain activities. Throughout the audit there are many opportunities to exercise sight, hearing, touch, and smell to evaluate a wide range of things. Observation is useful in most parts of the audit.

Inquiries of the client: Inquiry is the obtaining of written or oral information from the client in response to questions from the auditor. When auditor obtains evidence through inquiry, it is normally necessary to obtain further corroborating evidence through other procedures.

Mechanical accuracy: Testing of mechanical accuracy involves rechecking a sample of the computations and transfers of information made by the client during the period under audit. Rechecking of computations consists of testing the client's arithmetical accuracy. The mechanical checking in the form of test can be called as reperformance procedures.

Analytical Procedures: Analytical procedure use comparisons and relationships to determine whether account balances appear reasonable. The auditor's own calculations generally constitute the information used for analytical procedures. Analytical procedures should be performed early in the audit to aid in deciding which accounts need no further verification, where other evidence can be reduced, and which audit areas should be more thoroughly investigated.

Relationship of Evidence to Audit Risk

Several aspects of risks are directly related to the audit of financial statements. Two primary types are audit risk and business risk.

Audit risk is the risk that the auditor will conclude that the financial statements are fairly stated and an unqualified audit opinion can therefore be issued when, in fact, they are materially misstated. Business risk, in this context, is the risk that the auditor will suffer harm because of a client relationship, even though the audit report rendered for that client is correct. Audit risk can be represented by audit risk model. The business risk can be discussed in terms of auditors' legal liabilities as in the earlier discussion made in the previous section.

Audit Risk Model: The discussion on audit risk model emphasizes mainly on the various components of the model and their relationship to evidence requirements. The primary form of the model from the SASs is as follows:

$$DAR = IR \times CR \times DR$$

Where DAR = Desired Audit Risk

IR = Inherent Risk

CR = Control Risk

DR = Detection Risk

Desired audit risk: A measure of how willing the auditor is to accept that the financial statements may be materially misstated after the audit is completed and an unqualified opinion has been reached.

Inherent risk: A measure of the auditor's expectation that an error exceeding a tolerable amount exists in a segment before considering the effectiveness of internal accounting controls.

Control risk: A measure of the auditor's expectation that errors exceeding a tolerable amount in a segment will not be prevented or detected by the client's internal control structure.

Detection risk: A measure of how willing the auditor is to accept that the audit evidence to be obtained for a segment will fail to detect errors exceeding a tolerable amount, should such errors exist?

The Relationship of Audit Risk to Evidence

Using the audit risk model, there is a direct relationship between *desired audit risk* and detection risk, and an inverse relationship between desired audit risk and planned evidence. For example, if the auditor decides to reduce desired audit risk, detection risk is thereby reduced and planned evidence must be increased. The auditor must evaluate the preceding factors and decide on an appropriate *inherent risk* factor for each segment of the audit with evidence. Understanding the internal control structure, assessing *control risk*, and their impact on evidence requirements are so important. A specific approach that many auditors use to operationalize the use of *detection risk* to determine the amount of audit evidence to gather is statistical sampling.

Self-learning Activity

Try to answer the following questions on your own:

1. Describe audit-planning process;
2. Explain the relationship of audit evidence to audit risk.

Summary

- There are some types of audit evidence and working papers. There is relationship, both direct and inverse, of audit risk to evidence.

5 Audit Planning

Audit Planning Process

Audit Planning

The first generally accepted auditing standard of fieldwork requires adequate planning.

The work is to be adequately planned and assistants, if any, are to be properly supervised. There are three main reasons why the auditor should properly plan engagements: to enable the auditor to obtain sufficient competent evidence for the circumstances, to help keep audit costs reasonable, and to avoid misunderstandings with the client.

Obtaining sufficient competent evidence is essential if the CPA firm is to minimize legal liability and maintain a good reputation in the professional community. Keeping costs reasonable helps the firm remain competitive and thereby retain its clients, assuming the firm has a reputation for doing quality work. Avoiding misunderstandings with the client is important for good client relations and for facilitating quality work at reasonable cost.

Audit Planning Process

Audit planning process involves six stages: preplanning, obtaining background information about the client, obtaining information about the client's legal obligations, assessing materiality and risk, understanding the internal control structure and assessing control risk, and developing an overall audit plan and audit programme. Each of the first five parts is intended to help the auditor develop the last part, an effective and efficient overall audit plan and audit programme. The following figure depicts a clear picture on various stages of audit planning process, followed by discussion on each stage.

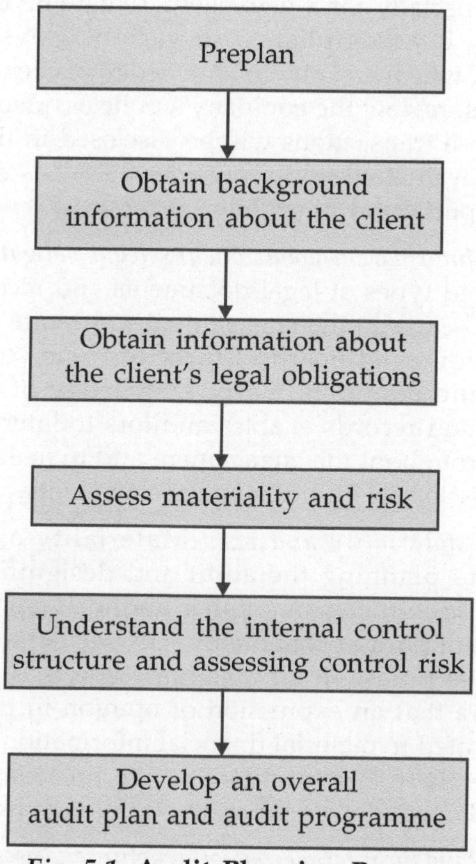

Fig. 5.1: **Audit Planning Process**

Preplan: Most preplanning takes place in the engagement, frequently in the client's office, to the extent that this is practical. Preplanning involves deciding whether to accept or continue doing the audit for the client, evaluating the client's reasons for the audit, selecting staff for the engagement, and obtaining an engagement letter.

Obtain background information: An extensive understanding of the client's business and industry and knowledge about the company's operations are essential for doing an adequate audit. Most of this information is obtained at the client's premises, especially for a new client. Obtaining background information is accomplished in various ways, the most important of which are: obtain knowledge of client's industry and business, review the company's policies, identify related parties, whose transactions will be disclosed in the financial statements, evaluate need for outside specialists in situations where the specialized knowledge is required.

Obtain information about client's legal obligations: Three closely related types of legal documents and records should be examined early in the engagement: corporate charter and byelaws, minutes of board of directors' and stockholders' meetings, and contracts. Early knowledge of these legal documents and records enables auditors to interpret related evidence throughout the engagement and to make sure there is proper disclosure in the financial statements.

Assess materiality and risk: Materiality and risk are important to planning the audit and designing the audit approach. The opinion paragraph in auditor's reports includes two important phrases that are directly related to materiality and risk. The phrase in all material respects is intended to inform users that an expression of opinion in the auditor's report is limited to material financial information. The phrase risk implies there is some risk that the financial statements are not fairly stated even when the opinion is unqualified.

Understand the internal control structure and assessing control risk: The study of the client's internal control structure and the resultant assessment of control risk are important to auditors and are specifically included as a generally accepted auditing standard. The second standard filed work deals with this. Management typically has five concerns in designing an effective internal control structure: providing reliable data, safeguard assets and records, promote operational efficiency, encourage adherence to prescribed policies, and comply with the foreign corrupt practices act. The assessment of control risk can be done by the steps: identification of control objectives, identification of specific controls, identification and evaluation of weaknesses, control matrix, assessment of control risk, and communication of reportable conditions.

Develop an overall audit plan and audit programme: The first five steps in the planning process are primarily for the purpose of helping the auditor develop an effective and efficient audit plan and audit programme. The audit programme is discussed in detailed manner hereunder:

Audit Programme

If audit is to be efficient it is necessary that it should be carried on regularly according to a definite programme. Audit programme is a scheme setting out in details the different phases of work to be done in the course of the audit it helps the auditor to carry on his work in a methodical and planned way. It is however, not a rigid programme. It needs modifications from time to time. Modifications are made in the light of experience.

Audit programme is not only scheme of work but also a diary of work. The different phases of work that are covered up are marked then and there in the programme. It serves many beneficial papooses. If facilitates audit a diary of work but also a diary of work. The different phases of work that are covered up are marked then and there in the programme.

It serves many beneficial purposes. It facilitates audit it helps to co-ordinate the activities of different members of the audit staff it enables the auditors to find out at any time what has been done and what remains to be done. It also acts as a source of information to the new members of the staff to gage the nature of work, which they are expected to do.

However, it has an obvious evil effect. It may sap the initiative of subordinates. Their work may lapse into a mechanical routine as they are simply expected to do their work as per the directions given in the programme. But taking suitable precautions may avert this danger. Subordinates should be given opportunities for manifesting their originality. They should be encouraged to suggest additions and modifications to the scheme. They should be trained to do their work intelligently.

Method of Work

The method of work to be adopted in conducing audit cannot be rigid. No hard and fast rule can be laid down recording the same. It will vary according to the capacity and experience of the auditor and the circumstances of the particulars cases. However, certain general points (which may form the basis for planning one's own method) may be laid down as under:

- Special and distinctive 'ticks' for different items (say, one for casting-forwards, third for postings ad so son) may be adopted. They should be very neat and small, and they should not overlap the figures.
- The meaning and significance of the different types of ticks should not be revealed to the clients and their staff: nor they should be allowed to use similar ticks.
- The audit staff should not enter into discussions with the employees of the business regarding the audit work, such discussions may be taken advantage of by them in ascertaining the weak points in the system of audit which might provide loopholes for concealing their frauds.
- In order to identify the entries of different periods different colour inks may be used for making 'ticks'.
- When calling back figures for the purpose of checking postings, the person who reads out should speak clearly so as to avoid the mistakes that would creep in one account of ambiguous pronunciation.

- All alterations and bad figures should be examined carefully and correct figures should be taken both in casting the original record and in posting to the ledger account.
- The bad practice of erasing figures with knife or rubber should not be allowed on any account.
- Special ticks should be used for altered items so as to see after wards whether alterations were made before or after they were ticked. Altered items can be dealt with in another way also. That is, correct figures may be written against the corresponding altered and unclear figures.
- As far as possible, examination of books should not e commenced before they are completely written up for the period.
- Entries made in pencil should not be checked at all.
- Entries made in pencil should not be checked at all and the stage to which checking is done should be take note of.
- While examining the postings, after the checking is over, the auditor should go through the items once again to find out if there are any unticked items. If so, they should be carefully examined.
- Checking of castings though a mechanical work by its very nature should be done with care and tact. The best thing is to total afresh and compares the result with the total appearing in the book.
- Preventive measures should be taken to obviate is of books being tampered with during the course of audit.

It is essential that the method of work to be adopted should be in conformity with the needs of the particular case and should be easily practicable.

Audit Notes and Working Sheets

Opinions may differ as regards the nature of notes to be taken during audit. But one thing is definite. That is, the labor involved in taking notes should be commensurate with the benefit likely to be derived there from.

Notes should be made of the following points:

1. The technical terms used in the business;
2. Accounting method followed in the business;
3. All important errors that are detected;
4. Various questions raised during the course of audit;
5. Explanation and information's received;
6. The particulars of missing vouchers, invoices etc.;
7. Matters that have to be remembered from one visit to another;
8. Points which need discussion with the authorities, and
9. Points to be incorporated in the audit report.

However unimportant questions an errors should be settled and adjusted then and there and there is no need to make note of them. During the first audit of a business which is of a technical nature, explanatory notes may be made of all kinds of transactions involving technical difficulties. These will be of good reference and guidance to the successors.

It is desirable to get all working sheets, drafts of accounts and other statements filed and kept safely. Audit notes and working sheets would be of great help which at a subsequent date it is found that something has gone wrong and the auditor it is called up on to explain and defend his position.

Working Papers

According to SAS 41 (AU 338), working papers are the records kept by the auditor of the procedures applied, the tests performed, the information obtained, and the pertinent conclusions reached in the engagement.

Working papers should include all the information the auditor considers necessary to conduct the examination adequately and to provide support for the audit report.

The overall objective of working papers is to aid the auditor in providing reasonable assurance that an adequate audit was conducted in accordance with generally accepted auditing standards. More specifically, the working papers, as they pertain to the current year's audit, provide a basis for planning audit, a record of the evidence accumulated and the results of the tests, data for determining the proper type of audit report, and a basis for review by supervisors and partners.

Contents and Organization of Working Papers

Each CPA firm establishes its own approach to preparing and organizing working papers, and the beginning auditor must adopt his or her firm's approach. The working papers contain virtually everything involved in the examination. There is a definite logic to the type of working papers prepared for an audit and the way they are arranged in the files, even though different firms may follow somewhat different approaches. The working papers start with more general information, such as corporate data in the permanent files, and end with the financial statements and audit report. In between the working papers are supporting the auditor's tests.

Working Papers Types

The type of working papers may vary or differ from one firm to another as discussed in the earlier paragraph. The working papers may be in the form of the following.

Working papers type include permanent files, audit programmes, general information, internal control structure, tests of transactions, analytical procedures, assets, liabilities and equity, operations, legal letters/contingent liabilities, adjusting journal entries, working trial balance, statements and audit report, etc.

Self-learning Activity

Try to answer the following questions on your own:

1. Describe audit-planning process.
2. What is audit programme?
3. Discuss the method of audit work.
4. Write short notes on: Audit notes and working sheets.

Summary

- Audit programme is a scheme of detailing the different aspects of work to be done during the course of audit process.
- Auditors are expected to prepare auditing notes and working papers to maintain important points during the course of audit.

6 Internal Control

Meaning and Definition

Internal control refers to the whole system of control employed by the management in the conduct of the business. It includes internal check, internal audit and other devices of control. Its efficient working in practical terms is helpful not only for the management but also for the external auditors.

Definition

The Committee on Auditing Procedures of the American Institute of Certified Public Accountants has defined 'internal control' as the plan of organization and all of the coordinate methods and measures adopted within a business to safeguard its assets, check the accuracy and reliability of accounting data, promote operational efficiency and encourage adherence to prescribed managerial policies.

Objectives of Internal Control

Internal control comprises all the methods followed by an organization and thereby:

1. Ensures efficient conduct of the business and prevents wastage;
2. Minimizes occurrence of fraud and error or irregularity, if not completely eliminated;
3. Protects its assets against improper disbursement;

4. Assures the high degree of accuracy and dependability of all the financial and operating information;
5. Judges operating efficiency and highlights weaknesses; and
6. Above all, measures the adherence to established policies of the company.

Internal Control and the Auditor

Before starting the audit, the auditor should review the system of internal control for the following considerations:

1. To examine the weakness of system, if any;
2. To consider the proposition of introducing test check to be performed during the course of audit; and
3. Based on the first and second considerations determine exactly the extent of work to be performed so as to enable the auditor to express his opinion on the given set of accounts.

Internal Check and the Auditor's Position

In small concerns where the volume of transactions is very little, it is possible for the auditor himself to go through every bit of detailed checking and to find out easily frauds and errors . But in the case of large undertaking having large volume of business, the auditor could not find much time for routine checking. In such cases, errors and frauds may easily scrape his notice, unless there is a certain internal agreement for countersinking. Such a system is called 'internal check'.

Internal check may be defined as mode of distributing the work among the various members of the staff in such a way that another of the staff independently counterchecks the work of each member.

Arnold W. Jhonson defines this system as one where in the accounting work of one employee is complemented and verified by the work of another employee both employees working independently and with out duplication of each others work objects.

The objects of instituting a system of internal check in a large business are:

(i) to ensure accurate record of all business transactions;

(ii) to lesson the chances of occurrence of frauds and errors; and

(iii) to relieve the auditor of a certain amount of routine checking.

In order to original a good system of internal check, it is necessary to fix precisely the duties and responsibilities of each member of the staff and to allocate the work among them such in a manner as a ensure automatic mutual checking on one another work. It is also desirable to maintain a perfect co-ordination among and linking of he different actions to enable the work as a whole to be carried out efficiently without any friction. A system of self balancing ledgers, automatic tills for checking cash receipts and time recording clocks for checking wages may be made to form part of the internal check.

Internal Check and Internal Audit

Internal check should not be confused with internal begin audit. Internal audit is entirely different from internal audits is entirely different from internal check. While the former is an independent examination of accounts by a separate staff employed for the purpose the latter is simply an internal arrangement among the members of the staff engaged in keeping accounts. Internal audit is virtually an audit. But internal check is only a device for counterchecking of one another work. While internal audit is complementary to regular audit internal check is merely preparatory to the same.

Advantages

Internal check helps to lighten the burden of the auditors work as regards detailed checking and he is enabled to bestow more attention to matters of importance. If the system is efficient and proper, chances of extensive frauds taking place would become remote. However, it cannot be laid down that internal check could make fraud impossible by all means. It only makes the occurrence of fraud more difficult and the possibility of its detection much earlier.

Auditor's Position

Where is an internal check in force, the auditor should firs examine the whole system. He should study the manner in which the duties and responsibilities were assigned among the members of the staff. He should satisfy himself that the system is not only good in itself but also carried out efficiently in practice by checking here and there at random. He should note the weaker points, if any, and devote special attention to them while examining the accounts. If he finds that the system is efficient; he may rely upon it to a certain extent and devote his attention to the important aspects or audit. The extent to which he may rely upon it depends on the circumstances of the particular case and this has to be decided by him. In this respect he requires 'considerable skill experience and judgment'.

Distinction Among Internal Audit, Internal Check and Internal Control

Internal audit: It is an independent appraisal activity within an organization to review the operations and records as to service for management and is done by specially assigned staff.

Internal check: It means a system under which the work relating to carrying out and recording of transactions is arranged in such a manner that another automatically checks the work of one staff member.

Internal control: By internal control, it means not only internal check and internal audit but the whole system of controls — financial and otherwise, established by the management in the conduct of business in an orderly manner, safeguard it assets and maintain the accuracy and reliability of its operations and records.

Internal Audit and External Audit

Internal Audit

Internal auditing is an independent appraisal activity within an organization for the review of operations as a service to management. It is a managerial control, which functions by measuring and evaluating the effectiveness of other controls.

External Audit

External audit is a statutory audit where the undertakings are formed under the statute or laws, in such undertakings audit is made compulsory under the statute. An external auditor does this.

Difference Between Internal Audit and External Audit

The following table depicts a clear picture on the difference between internal audit and external audit:

	Point of difference	Internal Audit	External Audit
	1	2	3
1.	Appointment of Auditor	By management	By the shareholders
2.	Nature	It is a staff function; the internal auditor may be an employee of the company	It is a line function; Auditor is an outsider
3.	Qualifications of the auditor	Need not possess as per the Act	Must possess qualification
4.	Major concern	Serving the needs of management	Compliance of statutory requirements

(Contd...)

	1	2	3
5.	Objective/basic function	Review operations and internal controls for developing improvements and ensuring compliance of policies and procedures.	Expression of an independent opinion on financial statements.
6.	Scope of work	Determined by management	Determined by Statutes
7.	Compulsion	Not compulsory	Compulsory in case of a company
8.	Reporting	Reporting to the management	Report is submitted to the shareholders in general meeting
9.	Span of checking	Checking of all the transactions take place	Test check may be applied.
10.	Removal of auditor	Can be removed by the management or board at any time	Can be removed by the shareholders
11.	Right to attend meeting	Has no right	Enjoys such right.

Self-learning Activity

Try to answer the following questions on your own:

1. What do you mean by internal control?
2. What is the position of the auditor as regards internal check?
3. Differentiate between internal audit and external audit.

Summary

- Internal audit is an independent appraisal activity within an organization to review the operations and records as to service for management and is done by specially assigned staff.

- Internal check means a system under which the work relating to carrying out and recording of transactions is arranged in such a manner that another automatically checks the work of one staff member.
- Internal control means not only internal check and internal audit but the whole system of controls.

7 Audit of Cash Transactions

Audit of Cash Transactions

The first book that is taken up for vouching is the cash book. Cash book is the most important subsidiary book. All transactions ultimately resolve themselves into cash transactions under double entry system of book keeping. It is kept for recording cash transactions only. In single entry system cash book is the only book of original entry in which are recorded all transactions irrespectively of their nature.

Majority of frauds generally arise directly in connection with cash in hand, therefore, the vouching of cash book should be taken up after a careful examination of the system of internal check if any, in vogue respecting cash transactions.

Internal Check as Regards Cash Transactions

As regards the mode of internal check for cash receipts and payments, no hard and fast rule can be laid down. The set-up of the system depends on the availability of sufficient number of members of staff and the volume and frequency of cash transactions. If sufficient number is available, each part of the work can be entrusted to one individual and the actual distribution of work can be made in such a manner as to ensure automatic counter-checking over one another's work. The best system is one which provides no loopholes to suppress receipt of cash or to create fictitious payments. A general procedure which could be adapted and adjusted according to the needs of circumstances may be outlined as under:

(A) *Receipts*

1. Cashier should not have any control over any ledgers or book of original entry excepting cash book. This is necessary for depriving him of the opportunity to make fraud lend entries with a view to conceal misappropriation of cash.
2. Receipt books not in immediate use should be kept under the safe custody of a responsible officer other than the person authorized to sign the receipt.
3. Daily letters should be opened in the presence of a responsible person and cheques, postal orders, etc., revived should be noted by him in a special register maintained for the purpose, they should be crossed and also marked 'account payee only'. This arrangement will rob cashier of opportunity for concealing or temporarily misappropriating receipts.
4. Entries for remittances of cheques and cash should be made by one person and they should be paid in to the bank by another. The clerk in charge of remittance should not have any other connection with the cash transactions.
5. All receipts should be banked daily.
6. Receipts prepared by the cashier should be counter-singed by another responsible officer before they are dispatched to the parties concerned
7. Cash book balance should be reconciled with pass book balance at regular frequent intervals.
8. An efficient system of internal check should be maintained as regards cash sales.
9. The preparation and dispatch of monthly statements of accounts of customers should be under the control of some responsible person other than the cashier.

(B) *Payments*

1. Inward invoices should be verified with corresponding order and checked before they are passed for payment.

2. All payments except petty items should be made by cheques.
3. Cheques issued should be crossed and marked 'not negotiable'.
4. The dispatch of cheques should be under the control of a responsible person.
5. Receipts received from parties to whom moneys are paid should be examined by a responsible person other than the cashier as to their genuineness and they should be regularly filed.
6. Monthly statements of account received from creditors should be reconciled with corresponding ledger accounts and if any discrepancy is noticed, it should be settled immediately.
7. An efficient system of internal check should be adopted as regards payment of wages.

The object of the system — the object of having an efficient system of internal check respecting cash transaction is two-fold the first is to ensure that all receipts of cash are correctly accounted for without any misappropriation. The second is to see that no false or over payments are made and every payment is a bonafide business expense.

The auditor should enquire carefully in to the system of internal check so as to satisfy himself that system is a proper one and carried out efficiently. On the basis of the facts of his investigation and his past experience, he should draw up plan for audit of cash book. he should bestow special attention to the weak points which he noticed in the system if he feels that the systems is not efficient, he should try to mend it by giving proper advice to his clients and by drawing their attention to its weakness and defects.

Vouching of Receipts

The vouching of the receipt side of the cash book is more difficult than that of the payment side since the available evidences in support of the receipt items are costly, internal the counterfoils or duplicates of the receipt book constitute the main source of evidence as regards the receipt of money from parties. In the case of withdrawals from the bank pass book entries and counterfoils, of cheques will be the evidence in this connection, it may be pointed out that carbon duplicates are preferable to counterfoils.

The evidences either in the form of receipts or in the form of entries in the case of withdrawals from the bank. Pass book entries and counterfoils of cheques will be the evidence in this connection, it may be pointed out that carbon duplicates are preferable to counterfoils.

The evidences either in the form of receipts or in the form of entries in the pass book should be vouched with the entries made on the receipt side of the cash book. The auditor should also see that the signature of the remitter obtained in every receipt wherever possible in the case of receipts through post the conversing letters should be examined if should also be seen that necessary precautions are taken to evidences and documents should be examined to ascertain the different sources of receipts and to ensure that all of them have been actually accounted for. Where a rough cash book is kept, it should be checked with the cash book. The following are some of the important items of receipts:

(*a*) *Cash sales* — this item provides great scope for misappropriation of money unless there is a definite system of internal check as regards the same. The best thing is to see that the salesmen do not receive cash, but simply make out the bills upon which money is paid to a desk cashier at the end of the day the totals of the duplicate bills in the hands of salesman should agree with the total of the daily sales book maintained by the desk cashier. Where there is such a system the auditor need not check all the bills. But he should verify the daily sales book within the bills at random. The castings of the book as well as the postings of the daily totals to the cash book should be checked. Where automatic tills are in use the daily totals entered in the cash book should be checked with the till rolls.

(b) *Cash from debtors* — as regards the receipt of cash from debtors the best precaution is to see the cashier has no control over the preparation or dispatching of the monthly statements to them. If any amount of receipt from a debtor is misappropriation will be brought to light when the debtor reports the discrepancy. Apart from comparing the entries on the book with corresponding receipts, the auditor should also verify the bills and cheques register and the copies of the statement of account sent to the debtors to satisfy himself that all items of receipts have been duly brought in to the account.

(c) *Receipt of loans* — a business concern may receive loans from financial institutions like banks and corporations for the purpose of its improvement and expansion. These items should be verified with the receipts the copies of loan applications if any the intimations of the sanction of the loans and other correspondences connected with the same. It should also be seen that proper sanction of the competent authority had been obtained for getting such loans.

(d) *Loan repayments by borrowers* — This is an important item of receipt in the case of banks and other financial institutions. It should be verified with the duplicates of counterfoils of the receipts on which the respective remitters have put their signatures.

(e) *Interest and dividend from investment* — a separate ledger account should be opened for each investment. The date when dividend or interest is due should be noted at the head of the account the auditor should see such ledger accounts and ascertain that all items of income receivable from investments have been brought in to account. Investments may consist of fixed deposits made in a bank shares and debentures of companies and government bonds income derived from them varies accordingly.

Interest received on deposits should be vouched with credit not received from the bank and with the bank pass book care must be taken to ensure that the pass book is genuine one. The correctness of the amount should be verified by checking the calculations in accordance with the terms of deposit.

Dividend received on deposits should be checked with the counterfoils of interest warrants.

Whenever investments are sold ex-dividend or bought cum dividend it should be seen that the dividends are subsequently received.

(f) *Interest on loan* — The counterfoils of the receipts issued to the borrower should be certified. The loan agreement or loan should be inspected it should be seen that interest provided for in it has been accounted for.

(g) *Miscellaneous receipts* — The items should be certified with the available evidences. The evidences may vary according to the nature of the transactions interest on current account allowed by bankers will be vouched with corresponding entries in the pass book. Commission received will be checked with the commission accounts rendered, and cash discounts with the credit notes received from the creditors. Rents receivable should be vouched by inspecting copes of leases and agreements and counterfoils of receipt book.

(h) *Extraordinary receipts* — in the case of extraordinary items, apart from the verification of concerned documentary evidences, the circumstances of the particular case should also be gone in to.

Receipts of subsidy from government may be one of such extra ordinary items in any of the business concerns which are under the 'protection' of the government. This should be verified with the order of the government granting the subsidy and the correspondences relating thereto.

Sales of fixed assets is also an extraordinary item this should be verified with the contractor sales and it should be seen that the sale has been made with the previous sanction of the competent authority.

Similar procedures may be adopted in the case of proceeds of the sales of investments. Amount received under insurance policy should be checked with the accounts rendered by the insurance company together with the concerned correspondence.

Remittance of money received besides vouching each item on receipt it should be checked whether the whole of money receive has been paid in to the bank promptly. This could be done by checking counterfoils of paying in book with the cash book.

Vouching of Payments

Every payment should be supported by a documentary evidence of good validity, i.e voucher. It should be a 'bonafied' transactions and should have been authorized by the proper authority. Documentary evidences for payments will generally consist of received from payees, acknowledgments cash bills band receipted accounts in vouching a payment item the relative voucher should be examined. The name of the payee, the date the amount and other particulars should be compared with the corresponding entries in the cash book the object of scrutinizing the dates is to guard against the production of vouchers of back years is support of fraudulent payments. The receipts from payees in their printed receipt form and those bearing their rubber stamp are better evidences than an invoice or account merely receipted in ink. It should also be seen that all receipts for amounts exceeding $.20 are properly affixed with revenue stamps. The audition stamp act, 1891 prescribes that stamp duty for receipts in respects of accounts exceeding $.20 shall be ten cents. The auditor will do better if he also examines the signatures in the receipts with those of previous receipts from the same parties to satisfy himself that no forgery is committed.

Some of the big concerns use cheques containing on the back suitable form or receipt. The discharged cheques are returned by the bankers to the clients and serve as vouchers for the payment. Where such receipted cheques are accepted as vouchers, the auditor should see that the names for the payee and the dates on the cheques agree with the names and dates in the cash book.

The name of the party to whom a voucher is addressed should be examined. It should be addressed directly to the business concerned. But if it is addressed to an individual such as partner, director or manager, care must be taken to ascertain that the payment relates to the business by examining whatever evidence available. If any such item is properly chargeable to individuals the auditor should ascertain that it is debited to the personal account concerned.

Payments to trade creditors — the receipts received from them should be examined. Where such payments are made by cheques, the counterfoils of cheque book and pass book entries should also be checked.

Distinction Between Capital and Revenue Expenditures

The distinction between capital and revenue expenditures is an important factor in vouching payments. Any wrong classification in this respect will vitally affect the final account revenue items are closed at the end of a period by transferring them to trading and profit and loss account and capital items are included in the balance sheet. So if a revenue item is treated as capital expenditure of vice versa both the final account and the balance sheet would be affected for example, if an amount of $.100 spent on repairs to buildings in wrongly debited to the building account, the value of the asset will be diminished to that extent resulting in inflation of profits.

Capital expenditure — Expenses incurred for the extension or improvement of an existing asset resulting in the enhancement of its revenue earning capacity may also be treated as capital expenditure.

Revenue expenditure — it is an expense which is incurred for carrying on the business and for maintaining the capital assets in an efficient working order, e.g., rent salaries wages, repairs renewals, etc.

The same kind of expenditure may be capital expenditure in one circumstance and revenue expenditure in another for example cartage incurred in the normal course of trading is classified under revenue expenditure, while cartage incurred on a newly acquired fixed asset like plant and machinery will form part of the cost of the asset and it should be treated as a capital expenditure. From this, it is clear that whether an item is a capital expenditure or not depends on the circumstances and the nature of business. (*See Table on next page*)

Vouching of Capital Payments

Much care should be bestowed up on vouching capital payments. the auditor should see that the payment is in order has been properly authorized and is a bonafide capital charge the important items of capital expenditure are as follows:

(i) *Plant machinery, furniture, etc.* — invoice and receipts should be examined enquiries should be made to ascertain the authentication of the expense. it should be seen that no repairs and expense of maintenance are added to the assets account however, the cost of direct expense which are incurred in connection with acquisition, like cartage or the cost of erection can be capitalized;

(ii) *Land and buildings* — if the land or the building was acquired by direct purchase the sale deed should be examined if the buildings are erected by the concern itself the contractors agreement tier receipts and engineers certificate should be verified the little deeds and conveyance should also be seen legal charges and engineers fee which form part of the capital outlay should be vouched with court receipts and engineers receipted accounts respectively;

The main points of distinction between *Capital Expenditure* and *Revenue Expenditure* may be summarized as under:

Capital Expenditure	Revenue Expenditure
1. It is incurred for the acquisition of a fixed assets or it may result in the creation of a fresh asset. For example investments made.	1. It is incurred not for creating an asset, but simply for the conduct of the business and for maintaining the capital assets in a state of efficiency. For example salary rent repairs.
2. It may increase the value of an existing asset for instance purchase of an additional building.	2. It does not increase the value of an existing asset.
3. It may improve the existing assets by enhancing their revenue earning capacity.	3. It does not in any way add to it earning capacity of existing assets but simply serve to maintain them in the original working order.
4. It may result in a reduction in the value of an existing liability for example refund of deposit and repayment of a loan.	4. It will only decrease the value of the total assets.
5. It will never be a loss to the business on the other hand it will mean either an asset or reduction of a liability.	5. It is a loss to the business since it represents a fresh payment out of the funds of the business without any prospect of its subsequent recovery.
6. It finds its place in the balance sheet.	6. It is transferred either to the trading account or to the profit and loss account.

(iii) *Investment* — the first care of the auditor in case of investments should be to see that they have been made on proper authorization of competent authorizes. For instance in the case cooperative societies investment are to be made in accordance with the providing of their by laws and the act and rules then he should verify the receipts for the payments made as well as the documents of title such as share certificates bonds etc where they have been bought through a broker his bought note should be examined;

(iv) *Loans* — in this case the loan application, the security offered, if any the sanction from the loan the bond and the acknowledgment of the borrower should be verified. In the case of mortgage loans the bonds should have been duly registered and encumbrance certificates obtained;

(v) *Patents* — the patent certificate should be examined. If it has been purchased the assignment should be inspected the fees paid to the patent agent should be checked with his receipted accounts;

(vi) *Payments under hire purchase and installment agreement* — the agreement should be examined. The vouchers for the payment of installments should be verified. The interest amount included in the installment should not be debited to the asset account.

Vouching of revenue payments

Usual revenue payments are as follows:

(i) *Wages* — this is a very important item in the case of large manufacturing concerns. First of all the auditors should see whether there is a through and efficient system of internal check for recording and payment of wages. He should examine the system and satisfy himself as to its thoroughness and strict observance in practice. He should check a proportion of the casings and calculations of the wages book and examine the weekly or monthly totals of the same with the cheques drawn as shown in the cash book. He should also compare the party roll with the time records in order to see that no 'dummy names' are included in it;

(ii) *Salaries* — the appointment file and the authority of appointment should be examined in order to ascertain the amount of pay, allowance, etc., and other conditions, if any. The amount of salaries paid to staff should be verified with the acquittance roll or salaries. Book in which the particulars of weekly or monthly salaries of very member of the salaried staff are recorded. The auditor should see that the amounts paid are in accordance with the scale fixed by the authority and that alterations in the scale, if any have been duly confirmed by that authority. It should also be seen that acknowledgments for amounts exceeding $.20 bear 10 cents revenue stamp;

(iii) *Freight and carriage* — the payments made should be vouched with the statements of accounts rendered by shipping or railway agencies together with corresponding receipts. It should satisfied that such payments were bonafide transactions by going through the purchases account for the actual arrival of the goods concerned;

(iv) *Contingencies* — contingent expense such as cleaning, lighting, rent etc., should be verified with corresponding vouchers or dockets. If these expense reinsured by the petty cashier they should be vouched with petty cash book;

(v) *Travellers commission and expense* — large commercial and trading concerns are engaging the services of traveling agents to push their sales in different places, and to collect money from debtors. These agents are paid either on salary basis or salary cum-commission basis. The commissions allowed and expenses met by them should be vouched with the accounts submitted by them. It should be seen that the amounts corresponded with the rates prescribed by the authority;

(vi) *Postage book* — postages are of small amounts but they provided ample scope for misappropriation if no efficient internal check on the same exists. The entries in the postage book should be examined with the dispatch register; the amounts drawn from the petty cashier by the despatch clerk should be verified and the balance on hand counted. It is safe, if the balance on hand is verified by surprised by some responsible person and reconciled with the book balance;

(vii) *Customs duties* — where these duties are paid through forwarding agents, the monthly statements and receipt received from them should be examined. The duties may be paid either in cash or through a current account opened with the customs authorities in the former case the receipts issued by the customs authorities should be examined. In the latter case the pass book entries and advices received from the authorities should be examined;

(viii) *Income tax* — income tax is payable on profits according to the provisions of the income tax act. The tax paid should be vouched with reference to the receipted challan of demand, assessment order and the copy of return submitted to the income tax officer. Income tax deducted from the employees salaries or wages should be vouched with the official receipts and challans and statement of deductions made. The total amount deducted during the year should be checked with the annual return;

(ix) *Sales tax* — sales tax is payable on sales either to the regional government or to the federal government. The amount paid must be checked with the receipted challans and returns submitted to the commercial tax authorities.

Internal Check as Regards Wages

Wages are paid to the labourers employed in the factory. There should be an efficient system of internal check as regards this item. The preparation of wage sheets and the actual payment of wages are two important operations connected with this item. Both of these should be done very carefully and systematically. The following system may be followed for the preparation of wages sheets and payment of wages:

1. There should be an organized wages office under the control of an officer other than cashier;
2. Workmen's record cards or book showing each workers date of birth, marital status, date of appointment, terms of employment, rates of pay etc. should be kept;
3. To enter the particulars of wages payable and paid to workers, wages sheets or books should be maintained. Separate sheets or books should be used for time workers and piece workers. They should contain columns for times of pieces rates of pay, gross amount payable, deductions for employees state insurance, provident fund contribution, income, tax, loans, fines etc. payment on account and the net amount payable;
4. The time of workers entering and leaving the shop should be recorded either by a gate keeper or time recording clock. In order to prevent loitering in the shop, the time of workers entering or leaving their departments should be recorded either by the respective foremen or by department time clocks;
5. The gate records and departmental time records should be compared by two clerks and any discrepancies enquired into;

6. The particulars of piece workers should be entered on piece work cards. When the work is given out, it should be recorded on the card. On completion, the card initialled by the piece workers and the foreman. The card should then be passed on to the wages office;

7. The times or pieces of each worker as the case may be, should be entered on the wages sheets by a separate clerk and the rates of pay inserted. The particulars of deductions should be then entered on the wages sheets. A separate clerk should calculate the net amount payable to each worker and enter it on the wages sheet. The calculations should be checked by another clerk. Each clerk should initial for the part of the work done by him. The sheets should then be countersigned by the works manager and passed for payment;

8. The wage sheets should then be handed to the cashier. He should draw and cash a cheque for the total net amount of wages payable. He should then place the amount due to each worker in an envelope bearing his name or number. The cash thus sorted should be handed to a responsible official for payment to workers. They will personally receive their wages the foremen should be present to identify the workers of their respective department. The wages of an absentee may be paid to another worker on production of his authorization letter. The cashier, the person paying the wages, the foremen, and the works manager, if present, should initial the wages sheets.

The Auditor's duty

He should examine into the system of recording and paying wages. If he finds it to be bad and defective, he should point out its defects and disclaim responsibility if the system is an efficient one, he need not check cash and every time in the wages sheets. He can check a proportion of calculations and castings he should vouch the total amount with the cheque drawn. He should see that the sheets have been initialed by all connected with them. He may also check at random the time records and piece work cards with the entries in the wages sheets. In order to ensure that no dummy names are included on the roll, he should call for the employees state insurance deduction cards and check the names in the wages sheets.

Vouching of Bank Pass Book

One of the important aspects of vouching of cash book is the checking of bank pass book with the corresponding entries in the bank columns of cash book (or bank account in the ledger). Pass book is nothing but a copy of the customers ledger account as maintained in the books of the bank. The individual items in the cash book should be called back with the pass book ticking the entries in both books. The reconciliation statement prepared at the end of the period to reconcile the cash book and pass book balances should be checked. The cheques paid in but not realized by the bank till the last day of the period under review and the cheques issued but not presented for payment until the date will not be found in the pass book as on that date. But it should be ascertained whether such items are bonafide transactions by going through the pass book of the succeeding period. It should be seen that the dates on the bank column of the debit side of the cash book agree with those of remittance columns of pass book except in he case of up country cheques which will be generally realized a few days later.

The counterfoils of the paying in slips initialed by the bank should be examined. It is more essential to ascertain that remittances have been made property and that there is no instance of 'splitting of cheques'. The splitting of cheques may be resorted to for the purpose of cancelling, misappropriation of cash received. For example, an amount of $.50 received from R.R. & Co., for $.50 and "S.S. & Co., $.50" in this way the original defalcation may be covered by subsequent splitting up of receipts for a certain length of time. Close study of counterfoils of the paying in slips with the pass book may disclose this sort of practice.

When checking the credit side of the cash book with pass book, the auditor should see that dates and names in both correspond and that all bank charges, dishonoured cheques etc., have been entered in the cash book. Auditor should not simply satisfy with the balance disclosed by pass book, since it is likely that dummy pass book might be produces to him. Therefore he should obtain direct from the bank, a certificate of the balance shown in the books of the bank as on the closing date of the periods.

Vouching of the Petty Cash Book

In large undertaking where there are numerous sundry items of small payments it is not worth while to record them in the main cash book. So a separate petty cash book may be maintained to record such sundry petty items.

A round sum sufficient to cover the estimated petty expense for a definite period say a week or month should be handed to the petty cashier by cheque. At the end of the period or earlier when his resources come to close, the petty cashier should balance his book and produce it to the cashier for perusal and verification. The cashier should vouch it and if it is in order, should give him a fresh cheque for the exact amount of the total disbursements for the period and thus restoring in his hands the original amount. This goes by the name of 'imprested system'.

The petty cash book should be ruled with analytical columns so as to save the number of postings to impersonal accounts. Vouchers must be obtained wherever possible for all payment. In such cases where it is not possible to get vouchers dockets must be made giving the details of the expense. They should be signed by the person who spent money. The amounts should be entered in them in works as well as in figures. They should be passed for payment by a responsible person no one other than the petty cashier should have access to the petty cash book. No money should be taken out of it for any purpose other than petty expense. No sums but the cheques specially drawn for the purpose should be utilized for petty cash.

As regards the duties of the auditor in respect of petty cash items, he should, at first enquire in to the system he should ascertain that the system is regularly carried out. if it is weak or faulty he should report the matter to the concerned authorities. The cheques drawn from the cash book should be vouched in to the petty cash book. The totals of the subsidiary columns of the latter should be cross cost and agreed with the total payments. The totals of debit side and the total payments column should be verified.

He should test check a certain portion of the vouchers carefully observing the nature of the payments and the heads of accounts if, in the course of that investigation, irregularities are notices he should purse his examination further and examine all the vouchers.

The postings of the total of the analytical columns to the impersonal ledger should be checked. It should be remembered that under analytical columnar impress system, there will be no petty cash account in the impersonal ledger and therefore, the balance of the petty cash book should be included in the trial balance.

The balance on hand should be verified by actual inspection. If it was held that the auditor has committed a breach of duty in not vouching the existence of petty cash balance. The best method to prevent the temporary misappropriation of petty cash amount by the petty cashier is to verify the cash balance of hand occasionally without previous intimation.

Self-learning Activity

Try to answer the following questions on your own:

1. How would the entries in the cash book be vouched?
2. What are the duties of an auditor in the case of missing vouchers?
3. How would you vouch the following items?
   (*a*) Cash Sales
   (*b*) Investments
   (*c*) Bank Pass Book

Summary

- In commencing a new audit, auditor should not get in to his work straightway. He should make a careful survey of all conditions relating to the work. He should make preliminary preparations before commencing his work.
- As regards the mode of internal check for cash receipts and payments, no hard and fast rule can be laid down. The set-up of the system depends on the availability of sufficient number of members of staff and the volume and frequency of cash transactions.

8 Audit of Trading Transactions

Vouching of Purchase Book

Trading transaction are dealings, which involve transfer of goods from one party to another. The transferor of goods is called the 'seller' and the transferee is called the 'buyer' trading transactions may be cash or credit transactions. With the development of transport services and credit mechanism, the volume of credit transactions has increased enormously. So much so 'without credit no business' is the slogan of the modern business world.

Again trading transactions deal with only such goods as are intended for resale, i.e., goods in which the business is carried on. This section deals with only credit trading transactions, since cash trading transactions merge themselves with cash transactions.

Purchases book is one of the various subsidiary records or journals maintained in a modern business. It records only transactions relating to credit purchases of goods, which are intended for resale. It is, thus a book of original entry for credit trading transactions 'bought day book' and 'purchases journal' are its other names.

Internal Check as Regards Purchases

As regards ordering and receiving of goods, a good system should prevail: otherwise, there would be more opportunities for fraud. Some such system as detailed below might be adopted. The storekeeper should prepare a requisition note or indent for the articles, the stocks of which are to be replenished. This requisition note should be endorsed by a responsible officer. On its basis orders should be made out in the order book which is printed in duplicate with serial numbers, the originals beings sent to the parties. When the goods are received the quantities and weights or measurements should be checked with the delivery notes and entered in the goods inward register kept at the godown. The calculations of the invoices should be certified by a clerk and their particulars should be compared with the goods in ward register and the order book. The prices should be compared with the quotations or previous invoices. Then the invoices should be passed for payment by the manager or any other responsible officer. The particulars of the invoices should be entered in the purchases book, the invoices being numbered and filed in the invoices file. The person in-charge of the purchases book should not be allowed to post the entries in to the ledger.

The auditor should study the system and devote more attention on weak points if any. He should check the invoices with the corresponding entries in the purchase book and cancel them after duly passing them when any suspicion arises, he should test the items of purchases book with the order forms and goods inward register. The calculations in the invoices should be test checked at random. When goods are purchased through the business for the personal use of the partners or directors or employees in order to get the benefits of trade discounts it should be seen that they have been debited to their respective personal accounts but not to the purchases account.

The practice of inflating profits by means of suppressing invoices might be restored to. Therefore, the auditor should go through the entries in the goods inward book for the last month of the period and trace into the purchases made during the last few weeks. He should, thus see if all such items recorded in the goods inward register actually appear in the purchases book for the period. If any item appearing in the goods inward register does not appear in the purchase book it would mean suppression of purchases. The invoice file for succeeding period may also be examined to see whether any of them should be charged to the current periods. If any of the purchases made at the end of the period were not transacted in the purchase book, it should be seen that such items were not included in the closing stock since such fraudulent inclusion would result inflation of profits.

Fraud might also be committed by means of entering an invoice twice in the bought day book in order to defalcate the amount of that item. Therefore auditor should take much care in examining vouchers with the entries in the purchases book.

Purchase Returns and Allowances

Purchase returns and allowances granted by the creditors in respect of goods rejected returned are entered in the returns Outward Book (or purchases Returns Book). When any goods are rejected and returned due to damages in transit, short weight or quantity or if there is any error in calculations, the matter will be brought to the notice of the concerned editor so that be can grant adequate allowance for the same. When the creditor signifies his consent to such allowances he will send a credit note. The Auditor should see that these items are properly dealt with. He should vouch the book with credit notes, Goods Outward Register (kept in the godown) and relevant correspondence. He should also check the castings and postings of the Book.

Hire and Instalment Purchases

First of all, the auditor should examine the actual Hire purchase agreement or agreement to pay by instalments and ascertain the particulars regarding the capital value of the property acquired, the rate of interest, the amount of instalment and the proportion in which that amount is to be apportioned between capital and interest. The vouchers for the payment of the instalments should be inspected. And it should be seen that proportionate interest has been charged to revenue but not debited to the property account.

Vouching of Sales Book

As regards executing the orders received for the supply of goods, some definite internal system should prevail. Order may be in the form of letters, travellers of agents of oral instructions. The particulars of every order, whatever may be its form should be entered in the Inward Order Book. When the orders are executed, invoices (which should be printed in duplicate with serial numbers) should be prepared and dispatched. From the carbon copies of such invoices, entries are passed in the Sales Book and they are posted to the respective accounts in the Debtor's Ledger. The details of goods sent out are checked with the invoices and recorder in the Goods Outward Register.

As regards sales, there may be two kinds of defalcations; viz, omission of sales and inclusion of false items of sales. The first kind of fraud would be detected by means of comparing the entries in the Sales Book with original records such as the duplicate invoices, orders and goods outward register. The second kind of fraud, viz, inflation of sales is often done with the object of inflating the profit improperly of decreasing the losses. This may be detected by the inspection of entries of the sales book with the original records with a view to ascertain that all items of sales book clerk should have no access to the Debtor's ledger.

The auditor should investigate the system adopted in executing orders for supply of goods. Invoices should be checked with sales book and the entries therein should be compared with the goods outward register. As regards sales during the close of the year, auditor should be careful enough to ascertain that items shown, as sales in the sales book were not included in the closing stock.

He should also see whether any items of sale of old assets have been passed through the sales book. If so, the amount of such items should not have been included in the total credited so the sales account, but credited to the asset account concerned. Auditor will do well, if he calls for statements of accounts from the Debtor's and compare them with the respective ledger accounts. This will prove to be an effective check up on the book debts and their collection.

Goods on Consignment

Occasionally, goods may be sent out by one trader to another for sale on commission basis at sole risk and account of the sender himself. Such sending- out of goods is called 'consignment'. The person to whom the goods are sent for sale is simply acting as the agent of the sender. The sender is called the consignor and the recipient of goods, the consignee. To the former it is an outward consignment, whereas to the consignee it is an inward consignment.

Usual procedure adopted in sending out goods on consignment is that the consignor dispatches the goods along with a Performa in voice in which a description of the goods, consigned and their cost or minimum sale price are given. From time to time, the consignee renders to the consignor, a statement of account known as 'Account sale'. The particulars of goods sold, the gross proceeds of the goods sold, the expenses incurred by the consignee including his commission and the net proceeds are set out in the account sales. Now let us see how accounts are maintained in consignor's books and also in consignee's books:

(*i*) *Consignor's book* — in practice, a separate consignment account is for each item of consignment with a view to ascertain its profit or loss. on the goods being sent out, the particular consignment account is debited with the invoice value of the goods and an account styled 'goods sent out on consignment' is credited any freight carriage insurance or other expenses incurred by the consignor on the consignment should also be debited to the consignment account. On receipt of account states from the consignee, the consignees account is debited with the amount of gross proceeds and the consignment account is credited. At the same time the consignment account is debited and consignees account is credited with the amount of expenses and commission deducted by him. The value of unsold stock, if any, is credited to the consignment. The balances of the consignment account will now represent either the profit and loss account.

Auditor's duty: the auditor should scrutinize carefully the consignment accounts. He should vouch the transactions and check the postings to consignment account. He should ascertain that the goods have been charged up at cost price. The account sales rendered by the consignee should be inspected. The incorporation of the particulars of the accounts sales in the consignment account should also be verified if at the time of balancing some portion of the consigned goods remain unsold in the hands of the consignee, the auditor should see that they are treated as stock on hand being valued at cost or market price whichever is lower in arriving at the cost price of such unsold stock the proportionate direct expense incurred by the consignor and the consignee may be added to the value of the goods. The auditor should make sure that no profit is taken credit for in respect of unsold goods.

Where consignments are charged at proforma invoice price plus a percentage above cost, the auditor should see that accounts are suitably adjusted at the time of balancing so as to have the same effect as if they were valued at the cost price.

(ii) *Consignee's books* — while auditing the accounts of a business where goods are received on consignment to be sold on behalf of the sender, the auditor should see that the sale of such items are treated entirely distinct from the ordinary sales effected by the business. A consignment inward register should be maintained to record the full particulars of consignments as and when received. No entries should be passed in any financial book until actual sales are effected if any expenses are incurred on behalf of the consignors, they should be debited to their respective accounts on sales being effected cash or partly account as the case may be should debited and the consignors account credited with the amount. As regards the commission due to the consignee, the amount should be debited to the consignors account and credited to the commission account.

The auditors should ascertain, by he inspection of contracts correspondence, proforma invoice, etc. the terms of the arrangement. The account sales submitted to the consignor should be examined with the consignment inward register and the consignors account in the ledger. It should also be seen that the statement of accounts received form the consignor is reconciled with the consignors account in the ledger.

Goods on Sale or Return

Goods sent out on sale or return can not be treated as actual sales until the customers have approved of the goods. Therefore they can not be passed through sales day book but be treated in a separate manner. These transaction may be treated in three different ways as detailed below:

1. Where such transactions are not very numerous, a sale or return book is issued it should contain columns for recording:

(a) the value of goods sent out;

(b) the value of goods sold; and

(c) the value of goods retuned.

In such a case only the amounts of the second column should be posted to the debit of the respective customers account in the sold ledger. The difference between total of the goods sent out column and the totals of the returns and sale columns taken together will represent the value of goods remaining in the hands of the customers. The auditor should examine the details of the sale or return book and check the postings from sales column on in to the sold ledger. The primary rule to be observed in these cases is that no credit should be taken for in respect of profit one sale until the sale is actually effected. The auditor should therefore ascertain that goods in the hands of customers unsold on the date of the balance sheet are valued at cost price and brought in to trading account and balance sheet as stock in trade.

2. Where the number of such transactions are numerous and the sums involved are large, the proper record of them demands the use of a separate set of books viz., a sale or return ledger. The sale or return journal and a sale or return ledger. The sale or return book which is in this case, ruled as an ordinary day book records all goods sent out on sale or return each personal account opened in the sale or return ledger is debited with the respective amount and the monthly total of this book is credited to 'goods sent out on sale or return account' in the same ledger.

   (*a*) The sale or return journal, then will contain columns for goods sold and goods retuned. When the goods are accepted by a customer, the particulars are entered in the 'goods sold' column of the sale or return journal. The amount is posted to the debit of the customers account in the ordinary sales ledger and to the credit of his temporary account in the sale or return ledger. The monthly total of this column is debited to goods sent out on sale or return account in the sale or return ledger and credited to the sales account in the general ledger.

When any goods are retuned the particulars of them are entered in the 'goods retuned' documents of the sale of retune journal each item is posted to the credit of the respective customers account in the sales or return ledger and the monthly total of the amount column will be debited to the 'goods sent out on sale or return account' in the same ledger the goods outstanding on sale or return on a particular date is represented by the balance of the "goods sent out on sale or return account" which should agree with the total of balance of personal accounts in the sale or return ledger. The auditor should vouch the sale or return day book and journal with the original records and check the casing and postings of these books. He should ascertain that the goods outstanding with customers on the date of balancing are valued at cost and treated as stock in trade.

3. Where is the quite unusual to send out goods on sale or return, such transactions are passed through the ordinary sales day book with a footnote that they are sent out on approval. Thus they are treated as sales on the goods being retuned, they are passed through returns inwards book and the customers account in the sold ledger in credited wit the amount.

Under these circumstances, the auditors should call for a schedule of goods. In the hands of customers and see that adjustment entries debiting sales account and crediting debtors on sale or return account with the total of such items are passed. The latter account should be taken in to the balances sheet and shown by way of deduction from sundry debtors. The value of the goods in the hands of the customers should be calculated at cost or under as the case may be and added to the value of stock in trade.

Sales Returns and Allowances

When goods are tuned to us the details of them should be recorded in the goods in ward register. Credit notes for the value should be prepared and dispatched to the customers concerned. The preparation and dispatch of these credit notes should be under the control of some responsible official who should sign them with reference to these credit notes, entries are passed in the sales returns book and posted to the credit note, entries area passed in the sales returns book and posted to the credit of the concerned customers accounts in the sales ledger (or debtors ledger) the auditor should check the sales returns book with credit notes corresponding debit notes received from the parties correspondence and goods inward register. It should all be seen if any such allowance relating to the period under review have been held back with the object of making the results shown by the trading and profit and loss account more favourable. This would be found by means of comparing the dates of credit notes and correspondences with those of entries in the sales return book.

Packages and Empties

This is one of the items which provide scope for misappropriation and therefore, the auditor should bestow great caution and care in vouching this item. In the cases where packages and empties are returnable by customers, they should be entered in the issue column of packages and empties register. When thy are actually returned, they should be entered in the recovery column of the register. Reference should be made in the register are regards the outward slips and inward slips for issues and recovery of packages respectively. at the time of balancing a reserve must be made for the value of packages and empties in the hands of customers at the same time creating adequate reserve for depreciation on the same.

When packages are charged out to customers, they need not be included in the sales but kept separately in a special column in the sales book. Auditor should verify such items with respective invoices.

If any packages and empties are sold outright to outsiders they should checked with the duplicate bills, in which the number of articles, the rate, the amount and other particulars should have been recorded. The auditor may also compare the rates at which the empties and packages have been sold with the prevailing market rates.

Self-learning Activity

Try to answer the following questions on your own:

1. How will you, an auditor, vouch credit purchase and purchase returns?
2. What steps should be undertaken by an auditor in vouching.
   (*a*) goods on sale or return;
   (*b*) consignment; and
   (*c*) packages.

Summary

- In commencing a new audit, auditor should not get in to his work straightway. He should make a careful survey of all conditions relating to the work. He should make preliminary preparations before commencing his work.
- As regards the mode of internal check for cash receipts and payments, no hard and fast rule can be laid down. The set-up of the system depends on the availability of sufficient number of members of staff and the volume and frequency of cash transactions.
- Trading transaction are dealings, which involve transfer of goods from one party to another. The auditor should check the respective vouchers and invoices.

9 Vouching of Subsidiary Books

It will not be out of place to trace briefly the evolution of subsidiary records in the modern accounting the main journal which was the only book of original entry in olden days is divided in to various journals which are called subsidiary records. Transactions of similar nature are passed through one separate subsidiary book. For instance, credit sale of goods are entered in the sales book and so on.

By means of such subsidiary records, such clerical labour is saved, since debit or credit for each item is not given in the ledger account, but only the monthly total of a subsidiary record is debited or credited in the impersonal ledger account for example, each individual credit purchase item is not debited to the purchases account in the ledger, but only the monthly total of the purchases book is debited to that account. Thus the evolution of subsidiary records has resulted in a labour saving device. In modern business houses the following subsidiary records are usually maintained:

1. *Cash book* — to record all receipts and payments of money;
2. *Purchases book* — to record credit purchases of goods intended for sale;
3. *Sales day book* — for recording credit sales of goods;
4. *Purchases return book* — to record the goods retuned to the suppliers;

5. *Sales return book* — to records the goods retuned by the customers;
6. *Bills receivable book* — to record the bills of exchange payable to the business;
7. *Bills payable book* — to record the bills to be paid by the business;
8. *Petty cash book* — to record petty disbursements.
9. Journal.

As regards the vouching of subsidiary records so far we have studied the vouching of cash book, purchases book sales book, purchases return book, sales return book and petty cash book. In this Section, the vouching of other subsidiary books is dealt with.

Bills Receivable Book

The particulars of all bills and drafts up on with the business is entitled to receive money at some definite future dates are entered in this book. The columns of this book will consist of:

(*a*) the date of receipt;

(*b*) from whom revived;

(*c*) by whom payable;

(*d*) the date of the bill;

(*e*) the term;

(*f*) the due date or the bill;

(*g*) amount;

(*h*) cash book folio; and

(*i*) how disposed of posting — each item is posted to the credit of the customers account, from whom the bill is received. And the monthly total of the amount column is debited to the 'bills receivable account' in the general ledger.

The auditor should vouch this book with the bills and other relevant correspondences, and should check the casting and postings also.

A bill may be disposed of in three different ways viz.:

(i) by discounting in the bank;

(ii) by transferring to a creditors; and

(iii) by realization of the proceeds on the date of maturity in the first case the auditor should vouch the proceeds with reference to the entries in the cash book and pass book.

It should be seen that the bank account is debited with the net proceeds, the balance being debited to discount account and the bills receivable account is credited with the full value of the bill in the second instance, the parties. Account and the bills receivable accounts credited with the full value of the bill in the second instance being debited the parties account receivable account credited with the amount. The auditor should compare the statement of accounts received form the creditors concerned with their accounts in the ledger and satisfy himself as to the genuineness of such transfers. In the third case, it should be checked with the cash book or pass book entry if the bill is dishonoured, its amount there of plus any expenses such as noting and protesting charges paid should be debited to the particular debtors account in the debtors ledger. The auditor should also inspect the bills on hand at the date of the balance sheet and see that the total of the amounts of such bills agree with the balance shown by the bills receivable account in the ledger.

Bills Payable Book

All bills accepted by the business in favour of its creditors are passed through this book. It contains suitable columns for recording the details of the bills. Each individual item is posted to the debit of the parties account for whom the bill is accepted and the monthly total of the amount column of the book is credited to the bills payable account in the general ledger.

This book should be vouched with reference to the concerned correspondence and parties accounts. As and when the bills are met they should be marked off in the how disposed of volume of the bills payable book. The payments made on bills should be checked with the corresponding retuned bills with acknowledgments. It should be seen that the total of the amounts of bills yet to be met, as shown by the bills payable book, is in agreement with the balance of the bills payable account in the ledger.

When a bill is dishonoured, the concerned parties account should be credited with the amount of the bills plus any expenses like nothing or protesting charges should be vouched with the relevant receipted accounts forwarded by the concerned creditors.

Journal

The use of the modern journal is very much restricted. It is recorded only the extra ordinary transactions, which could not be conveniently recorded in any other book of prime entry. The following transactions are generally entered in the journal:

(i) opening entries;

(ii) transfer from one account to another;

(iii) rectification of entries;

(iv) adjustment entries for outstanding, etc.

(v) closing entries, relating to dishonours of bills; and

(vi) such other transactions for which there is not special book of prime entry, as consignments, joint ventures, etc.

These items are evidently of great importance so far as they affect the final accounts. The auditor should, therefore, vouch thoroughly the entries passed in the journal, opening transaction like acquisition of assets from vendors should be checked with the respective contracts. In this way every item should be examined properly with the relevant documentary evidences. The postings should also be checked on the respective accounts in the ledgers.

Audit of Ledgers

Ledger is an all important book and it is the book of final entry. Every business transaction after passing through a book of original entry finds its ultimate place in the ledger. It is book of accounts. It gives all the necessary information regarding the working of the business in a properly arranged classified and condensed form it is nothing but a classified summary of the various books of original entry.

While examining the nominal accounts in the impersonal ledger, the auditor should carefully examine the particulars of each item in order to ascertain that postings were made under proper heads of accounts. For instance cartage incurred on goods purchased should be posted to 'cartage inward' account but not to the 'cartage outward' account because it is legitimate expense on purchases, which should be charged to Trading Account.

Similarly, while examining asset accounts, the Auditor should see that no item of a revenue nature like repairs, etc., is posted in them. The correctness of ascertaining how far the Balance Sheet reflects the true state of affairs of the concern depends mainly on the intelligence and thoroughness with which the impersonal Ledger is examined by the Auditor. He should know the meaning and significance of every item in the Ledger. He should study its truth, and satisfy himself that it is in order, properly classified and correctly posted in the proper account.

Self-learning Activity

Try to answer the following questions on your own:

1. What is the place of journal in modern book keeping? How could it be vouched?

2. How would you vouch bills receivable book and bills payable book?
3. Explain the method of checking various ledgers.

Summary

- Other subsidiary books like bills payable, receivable and journals are to be vouched by the auditor.
- Ledgers of different kinds and final adjustments are vouched and verified by the auditor with evidences.

10 Audit of Final Adjustments

In every business undertaking, at the time of periodical balancing, there may be several items which need adjustments for the purpose of bringing in to account outstanding liabilities and assets. There may be certain items of expenses, such as, rent, salaries, wages, etc., that belong to the period under review and have accrued, but have not been paid and, therefore, do not appear in the accounts. All such outstanding expenses should be brought in to account by passing adjustment entries. The amounts outstanding should be debited to the respective Nominal Accounts and the 'Outstanding Creditors Account' should be credited with the total. The latter will appear in the Balance Sheet under the liabilities side.

In contrast to these outstanding expenses, there may be expenses that are usually paid in advance, such as insurance, rates and taxes, etc. It so happens that, at the time of balancing, the whole of the period covered by the amount spent is not yet expired. That portion of the amount relating to the unexpired period should, therefore, be carried forward. This is done by debiting an account styled 'Prepaid Expenses Accounts' and crediting the particular Nominal Account with the unexpired portion of the amount.

Similarly, incomes accrued and due but not received at the time of balancing are brought in to Account by passing necessary adjustment entries. In this case, Outstanding

Debtors' Account is debited and the particular Nominal Account is credited with the amount to be received. The former Account is shown as an asset in the Balance Sheet. Incomes received in advance, if any, should be adjusted properly. Only such portion of an income as pertaining to the current period is transferred to the final account, the balance being carried forward.

The adjustment is made by debiting the particular Nominal Account and crediting 'Prepaid Income Account' with the amount received in advance. The latter Account is shown on the liabilities side of the Balance Sheet.

Final adjustment is as much important as the entries already appearing in the books. It is indispensable for arriving at the correct result of the business for a particular period. Under final adjustments are also included the bringing-account of the closing stock, writing-off of bad debts, making provisions for doubtful debts and depreciation on fixed assets.

Outstanding Liabilities

1. *Expenses due or pending payment:* The omission to bring any outstanding liability for expenses in to the accounts will affect the profit and Loss Account. The Auditor should, therefore, see that all outstanding liabilities for expenses for the period under audit are dealt with properly. The purpose of his investigation, in this respect, is to make sure that no liability is suppressed or concealed; the following are the common instances of outstanding liabilities.

2. *Wages:* In the case of a manufacturing concern, the amount of wages occurred after the date of the last payment during the period till the date of balancing should be calculated and provided for. The provision should be made by debiting the wages Account and crediting the Outstanding Creditors' Account with the amount of Outstanding wages is shown on the liability side of the Balance Sheet.

3. *Rent, Rates etc.:* The Auditor should examine the ledger accounts, demand notices and acknowledgements carefully noting the period covered by each payment and see that any accrued and unpaid amount to the date of the Balance Sheet is brought in as a liability.

4. *Salaries:* the Acquittance Roll or Salaries Book should be examined noting the period covered by the payments and it should be seen if the amount outstanding for the period has been provided for.

5. *Trade Expenses:* A schedule of sundry expenses pending payment for the period should be prepared and its total should be debited to trade expenses Account and credited to Outstanding Creditors' Account.

6. *Legal Charges:* Legal Charges relating to the period under review but not actually paid for the Solicitors should be ascertained with reference to the Solicitors' bills and correspondence and provided for.

7. *Auditors' fee:* The proper procedure to be adopted as regards the cost of Audit is that fee for the period under review should be provided for in the accounts of that period itself, even though, in practice, it is paid only in the succeeding period. If the amount of fee is not yet fixed, an estimated amount may be brought in as an outstanding liability.

8. *Interest payable:* Where there are any loans, mortgages, debentures etc., the interest due or accrued on them to the date of balancing should be calculated and provided for. This should be examined by the Auditor with reference to the loan agreements and the acknowledgements for interest actually paid.

9. *Incomes received in Advance:* It is essential to apportion any income received in advance and only the portion relating to the currents year should be brought in to the profit and Loss Account, the balance being carried

forward. Advertisement charges received by newspaper concern and insurance premium received by an insurance company may be cited as examples. The Auditor should examine such nominal accounts, noting the periods covered by them, and see that the amount pertaining to the unexpired period has been properly calculated.

Outstanding Assets

Outstanding assets may be classified under two broad heads viz.:

(i) incomes accrued and due; and

(ii) items of expenses paid in advance. Just as all outstanding expenses relating to the period are provided for, so also all incomes due and accrued at the date of balancing are brought in to account. However, it is reasonable that any outstanding income that is not likely to be received should not be brought in to the profit and loss account unless sufficient reserve is created for it.

1. Incomes due and accrued:

   (i) *Rent receivable* — All items of rent receivable from tenants due on or accrued to the date of the balance sheet should be calculated and brought in to account. This is done by debiting the outstanding debtors Account and crediting the rent receivable account with the calculated amount. The auditor should also see if adequate reserve for doubtful or irrecoverable arrears has been made.

2. Interest and dividend — interest accrued on loans advanced and investment to the date of the balance sheet should be calculated and brought in to account. In the case of items doubtful of recovery, adequate reserve should be created the adjustment entry should be verified with the reference to the bond and interest account. Similarly, dividends on shares and stocks may be

calculated brought in to account. This should be check with reference to the share certificates and dividend warrants.

3. Commission receivable — commission due are accrued to the date of the balance sheet should be brought in to account. the auditor should examine the basis of calculation in order to satisfy himself that the amount brought in to account is correct.
4. Payments made in advance — At the time of balancing there may be some items of expenses, such as rent, rates advertisement, insurance, etc., which are paid in advance, covering a period beyond the date of Balance sheet. The proportionate amount for the unexpired period should be calculated and carried forward to the next year. The Auditor should examine the adjustment entry as well as the vouchers for such payments and verify the calculations.

Deferred Revenue Expenditure

Revenue expenses of large amounts, the benefits of which are likely to accrue over a number of years beyond the year in which they were incurred are used to be temporarily capitalized and written off equitably during those years, e.g., Preliminary Expenses, Brokerage on shares, cost of Issue of Debentures and Discount on issue of Debentures. They are called Deferred Revenue Expenses. Every year the proportionate amount is charged to revenue and the balance is carried forward.

Regarding the audit of these expenses the Auditor should study the circumstances of each case and satisfy him that the amount carried forward is fully justifiable.

Alterations to Plant

Some times heavy expenditure may be incurred for improving plant and machinery or for adopting it to the changed conditions of trade. This expenditure improves the earning capacity of the business. There fore it is not wholly charged to current revenue. It is written off over a short period of years, where there is no repairs and renewal fund against which it may be debited.

The auditor should study the nature of the expenditure and examine the reasonableness of the period of years over which they expenditure is to be written off. If necessary he should refer to its treatment in his report.

Advertising

When a new business is established or a new product is introduced in the market, heavy expenditure on advertising is incurred. Such expenditure is a form of capital expenditure as it is a development expenditure. However it is not a permanent as set, and it is preferable to write it off over a period. Similarly when the advertising expenditure incurred in a year is abnormally heavy and if its benefit is likely to accrue over a period of years, it is written off over that period.

The auditor should verify the expenditure by examining vouchers, correspondences, etc., and see that it is not carried forward over an unreasonable length of time.

Depreciation, Reserves and Contingent Liabilities

Depreciation

Depreciation has been defined as a loss or diminution in the value of an asset on account of wear and tear, obsolescence or effluxion of time. In other words, it is a shrinkage in the use value of an asset. Shrinkage in value is a common phenomenon that would occur in all assets acquired for the purpose of being used in the business.

The cause for depreciation may be internal or external. Internal cause is natural to or inherent in the asset itself, e.g., wear and tear. Depreciation arises due to this cause in the case of such assets as plant and Machinery, Motor Lorries, Furniture and Fittings, Buildings etc. External causes are the manifestations of forces in operation outside the asset itself. Obsolescence and effluxion of time are important among them. An asset like a plant may become obsolete i.e., out of date due to invention of an improved type and consequently loses its used value. Depreciation is caused by effluxion of time in the case of assets like leases, which become valueless after the end of a definite period.

Depreciation is different from temporary fluctuations. There may be temporary diminution in the value of an asset due to fluctuations in market value. This temporary reduction-value is not to be considered as depreciation. It is not a shrinkage in use-value of the asset; it is only a probable loss in realizable value which would not affect, in any way, the earning capacity of the asset.

There prevails one misconception, which need clarification. It is contended that depreciation is an appropriation of profits and not a charge in the revenue. Therefore, it is said that no provision can be made for depreciation when there is no profit. This contention is a mere farce. It is an illusion but not a fact. It is contrary to reality. It is a fact that diminution in value of an asset due to causes like wear and tear or effluxion of time occurs irrespective of the results of business. As such, it is not contingent on the earning of profits. Thus depreciation is not an appropriation of profits but a legitimate charge on the revenue itself. It is an integral cost of conducting the business during the effective life of the asset and is not dependent on the amount of profit earned.

The Object of Providing for Depreciation

Depreciation is a legitimate charge that has to be provided for. Assets, which are in constant use, diminish in value on account of wear and tear. The use of an asset contributes to the earning of profits. But it results in the depreciation of the asset. Therefore, the loss in value in the form of depreciation should be treated as an expense in order to arrive at the true profits of a concern. Strictly speaking, the amount spent on the purchase of an asset is nothing but capitalized rent. Instead of hiring an asset and paying rent thereof, the asset is acquired for permanent use in the business and thus the rent is capitalized The proportionate charge is represented by its depreciation Accordingly, it is but natural that depreciation should be treated as an expense.

Moreover, if the diminution in the value of an asset is not provided for, the value of an asset would be overstated. There fore, if the Balance Sheet is to represent the true and correct view of the state of affairs of the business, the depreciation of the assets should be provided for.

Again, the capital invested in the acquisition of an asset is lost at the end of its working life. If the business is to run continuously this loss should be made good. But this can be done only by holding back a portion of revenue from time to time by means of providing for depreciation, which represents the proportionate loss of capital out-lay on the asset.

The object of providing for depreciation is, therefore, three-fold viz.:

(i) to arrive at the correct profit or loss;

(ii) to make the Balance Sheet represent the real state of affairs; and

(iii) to keep the capital invested in the acquisition of fixed assets intact. The proportionate loss in value of the capital is made good out of revenue at regular periodical intervals.

The Methods of Providing for Depreciation

The nature of assets is varied; their value is also varied. So also the methods of providing for their depreciation. The method of making provision for depreciation. Varies according to the nature and value of the asset and the need for replacing it at the end of its life. Whatever be the method selected, it should be applied consistently. Otherwise, the usefulness of periodic accounts for comparison of one period with another may be vitiated. As regards the provision for depreciation, temporary assets are to be treated in one way, permanent assets in another way and wasting assets in a third way. Whatever may be the method, certain general points are taken in to consideration in estimating the amount of depreciation to be provided for. The points are:

(*i*) the original cost of the asset;

(*ii*) its probable walls;

(*iii*) the break-up or residual value of the asset; and

(*iv*) the chances of the asset becoming obsolete.

The working life is not susceptible of precise calculation. The amount of depreciation provided for is therefore a matter of estimation, based on the available experience and knowledge, Rather than of accurate determination. It requires adjustments from time to time according to changes in experience and knowledge.

The cost of the asset less its 'scrap value' represents the net amount of capital outlay, which is lost during the course of its lifetime. The loss for a year, i.e., depreciation for a year can, now, be ascertained by dividing that net amount (cost less scrap value) by the number of years of its probable working life. This estimate should be revised from time to time in the light of experience so as to attain a fair accuracy. With this back-ground in view, we can study the various methods of provide-back-ground in view, we can study the various methods of providing for depreciation. The following are the principal methods:

(*a*) *The Fixed Installment or Straight Line Method* — It is the simplest of all methods. A fixed proportion of the original cost is written off each year so as to reduce the value of the asset to nil or break-up value at the end of its life. The amount to be written off by way of depreciation is constant from year to year and the value of the asset is reduced correspondingly. This method, thus, spreads the provision equally over the period of anticipated use.

Repairs and small renewals are charged to revenue. The method is suitable for simple assets like patents and short leases etc. It is used almost universally in U.S.A., Canada and England. It is considered to be the most suitable for general application.

(b) *The Diminishing Balance Method* — This method is different from the first one. Under the method a fixed rate percent on the reduced balance brought down on the asset account is written off every year. The amount of depreciation will not be constant and be lesser and lesser every year; say an asset worth $.10,000, is to be written off under this system at 10 per cent. In the first year, the amount of depreciation would be (10,000 x 10/100=) $.1,000, and the reduced value of the asset would be $.9,000. At the end of the second year, the amount of depreciation to be provided for would be (9,000 x 10/100=) $.900, and the reduced value of the asset would be (9,000_900=) $.8,100, Thus the amount of depreciation would decrease from year to year.

Under this method, the rate percent should be higher than that in the first method, since the amount written off diminishes each year. The percentage applied needs to be from two to three times that applied under the straight-line method. This method is more scientific than the first one. It is more advantageous in the case of assets which are subject to repairs such as plant and machinery. It is a fact that the cost of repairs increases as the asset grows older, but the amount of depreciation under Diminishing Balance Method diminishes every year. Accordingly, the total charge against revenue on account of both depreciation and repairs is equalized.

(c) *The Annuity Method* — Under the Annuity System, the amount spent on the acquisition of the asset is regarded as a capital investment earning a certain rate of interest. When an asset is acquired, not only the original cost but also the interest on its capital outlay is lost at the end of its life. So interest at a fixed rate calculated on the original value of the asset is debited to the Asset Account. The cost of the asset plus the amount of interest debited is written down annually by equal instalments.

Until it is reduced to zero or its residual value at the end of its life. The exact amount of installment suitable for each case can be ascertained from Annuity Tables. The system will not be suitable in the case of assets which involve periodical additions. But it can be applied to long leases where is no question of addition. However, some authorities are of the opinion that interest should not be taken in to account in calculating depreciation. My personal opinion concurs with such authorities. The amount spent on the acquisition of an asset is nothing but a portion of capital. When interest is calculated on capital, there is no need for Annuity Method. Otherwise it would mean double calculation of interest on the capital outlay involved in the asset.

(*d*) *The Depreciation* (*or Sinking*) *Fund System* — This system is an improvement over the Fixed Instalment System. It consists of not only providing for depreciation but also of creating funds for the replacement of the asset at the end of its life. An asset is utilized in the business for earning profits. By serving its purpose, it depreciates in value; it becomes useless at the end of its life when there is the need for the purchase of a new one. This requires large amount or capital. Sudden withdrawal of a large amount from the business would affect the financial position very much. So there is the need for setting aside a portion of the revenue every year so as to create adequate funds for the purpose of replacement of the asset without affecting the financial position of the business all of a sudden.

Under the Depreciation Fund System, the asset account is kept at its original value. A fixed amount is debited to the profit and loss Account each year and credited to 'Depreciation Fund Account'. An equivalent amount of cash is withdrawn and invested outside the business. This investment is allowed to accumulate at compound interest, so that adequate funds will be available at the end of the estimated life of the asset in order to replace it. The Investment Account is called 'Depreciation Fund Investment". This method is not widely used, except in public utility concerns.

(e) *The Revaluation Method* — this method is adopted in the case of assets that violently fluctuate in values and where the other methods cannot be adopted satisfactorily. Under this method, the asset is revalued at the end of every year; the difference between the book value and the amount of revaluation is debited to depreciation account and credited to the asset account if the revaluation figure is greater than the book value the difference would represent an appreciation which being of a temporary nature need not be brought in to account. This system is suitable for assets like live stock, loose tools, stock in trade etc.

(f) *The Insurance Policy Method* — This method in similar to depreciation found system. The purpose in the same in both cases i.e, to create enough funds for replacement. Under insurance policy method instead of investing the amounts in outside securities an endowment insurance policy for the estimated life of the asset is taken so as to produce the required amount for replacement at the end of the period. The premium is paid in yearly instalments.

In one respect, the insurance policy method is superior to the depreciation fund system in the former cases the amount of the fund created for replacement is certain and does not fluctuate but in the latter case the value of investment is liable to market fluctuations.

(g) *The Depreciation cum Repairs and Renewals Method* — Under this method is charged one single sum to cover repairs, renewals and depreciating the actual amount of repairs and renewals it transferred to the fund account.

The Application of the Methods to Different Assets

1. *Freehold land* — It does not depreciate. But it is subject to fluctuating in the case of permanent fall in value depreciation has taken place and may be provided for by adopting revaluation method. Temporary fluctuations are, in general not taken in to considerations.

2. *Good will* — Depreciation does not arise.

3. *Freehold building* — The amount of depreciation on freehold building is calculated with reference to its age and quality of its construction and the purpose for which it is used in the business. Repairs should always be charged to revenue though the depreciation fund system is preferable, the straight line method is usually adopted.

4. *Leasehold land and buildings* — The total cost of lease should be written off over its period in the case of buildings created on lease leased land provision should also be made for dilapidation claims that may be made after the termination of the lease. Where the value is small the fixed instalment system may be adopted. Where the lease is longer and the amount is larger, the annuity system may be adopted. Where there is the need for renewing the lease, the depreciation fund or insurance policy system should be adopted.

5. *Plant and machinery* — Plant and machinery depreciate on account of internal causes (i.e., wear and tear) as well as external causes, (viz., obsolescence) the reducing balance method is usually adopted . When the plant is heavy and requires replacement entirely, the depreciation fund or insurance policy method should be adopted when the possibility of obsolescence is great, the asset should be revalued at periodical intervals. Machinery bought on hire purchase system should be depreciated on the total cost and not on the amount of instalments actually paid.

6. *Loose plant and tools* — These are consumed in he course production. Therefore, the revaluation method is the best to be adopted.
7. *Furniture, fixtures and fittings* — The reducing instalment system is adopted, repairs being charged to revenue fixtures and fittings like partitions bookshelves electric wiring and fittings have no realizable value and therefore the entire cost should be written off during their estimated life.
8. *Patents* — depreciation arises on account of effluxion of time. It is granted for a period of 16 years. The value should therefore, be written off over a period of its official life. It may become obsolete or, it may not be possible to work it at a profit. In such cases revaluation is necessary. But in no case its value should be written up. Renewal fees paid for maintaining the patent should be charged to revenue. Fixed instalment system is preferable.
9. *Copyright* — this also suffers depreciation from effluxion of time. The term of copyright is ordinarily the life of the author and a period of fifty years after his death. A copyright does not ordinarily retain its value throughout its legal life so it needs revaluation year after year. Hence revaluating method is suitable.

The Auditor's Duties as Regards Depreciation

The auditor must remember the fact that the question of depreciation is closely connected with the balance sheet an auditor has no technical knoledge of such assets as plant and machinery so he cannot estimate the working live of assets of a business. But he should study the circumstances of each cases ascertain the accuracy of the estimation of the working lives of the assets. He should see that the rate per cent is sufficient to reduce the value of the asset is nil or scrap valued at the end of its life. The management should be fully consulted. The opinions and conclusion of experts should be accepted. If the auditor feels that the question of depreciation has not been scientifically considered and that the provision made is insufficient, he should point out the same in his report. His main responsibility is to satisfy himself that the amount of depreciation is both adequate and accurate. This duty is more important. If he neglects to do full justice to this part of his duty. He would be held guilty for negligence of duty and falsification of accounts.

Reserves

The word 'reserve' means holding back something for future. Business is a risky affair. Risks may be known or unexpected. Prudence requires that provisions must be made for future contingencies. Such provisions are called 'Reserves'. For the purposes of study, reserves may be classified into — General Reserve and Specific Reserve.

General Reserve: A General Reserve is a reserve created for general purposes without any specific object in view. A General Reserve may be defined as a sum set aside out of divisible profits and retained to provide for unexpected or unknown future losses or to accumulate additional working capital or to equalize dividends or to strengthen the financial position of the concern. In other words, it is a surplus created out of divisible profits. It is represented by the excess of assets over capital and liabilities. A General Reserve presupposes a profit; it cannot exist, side by side, with a debit balance of profit and Loss Account. It is therefore, an appropriation of profits. The existence of a General Reserve depends on the valuation of the assets. when assets are under-valued the reserve will not be visible. If assets are over-valued without making sufficient provisions for depreciation, then the General Reserve is fictitious and non-existent to the extent of such over-valuation. If a General Reserve is to be real, it must be a bonafide surplus of assets over capital and liabilities, the assets and liabilities being valued properly.

Auditor's duty — the creation or otherwise of a General Reserve is a matter of financial policy. It is to be decided by the managing authorities. The Auditor is not concerned with the same. Nor he has to worry himself as regards the adequacy of the amount. It is enough if he checks the accuracy of the accounting. However, there is one thing to be noted by the Auditor. A problem may arise whether to retain the reserve in the business itself or to invest it outside the business. The Auditor may be required to advise on this matter. This question depends on the financial requirements of the business. If it is in need of more working capital, the amount represented by the General Reserve may be profitably employed in the business itself. Where there is no such requirement, it is wise to invest the amount in gilt-edged securities outside the business.

Specific Reserve: A specific Reserve is created for definitely known purposes. It may be defined as a provision made out of revenue for some known or expected losses, such as, 'Reserve for disputed claims' In this case; the reserve should be charged to the profit and Loss Account. A Specific Reserve is a charge against revenue. It must be before the ascertainment of the net profit or loss. The provision is made before the ascertainment of the net profit or loss. It is not made after ascertaining the profit and Loss Account.

The term 'Specific Reserve' is rather misleading. It is better to use the term 'Provisions'. The following are some examples of Specific Reserves:

1. Provision for Bad Debts;
2. Provision for discounts;
3. Provision for depreciation on investments; and
4. Provision for insurance.

Auditor's duty — In the case of Specific Reserves, the Auditor has a specific responsibility. He should consider the adequacy of these reserves. If the amount provided for is not sufficient for the purpose, it should be pointed out by the Auditor. Otherwise, he would be held responsible for negligence of duty. He should examine the circumstances of each case and satisfy himself him self as regards the adequacy of the provisions. If he feels that the amount provided for is insufficient, he may try to persuade his clients to increase it. If he fails in his attempt, he should not hesitate to point out it in his report.

Secret Reserve: There is also another kind of reserve know as 'secret reserve'. Secret reserve as the very name implies is a general reserve, the existence of which is not disclosed in the balance sheet, so that the actual financial position would be better than what it appears to be on the fact of the balance sheet. Secrete reserve may, thus, be defined as a general reserve the existence of which is not apparent on the face of the balance sheet. It is the opposite of 'window dressing'. Its existence is an indication of the better financial position of the undertakings.

The object of creating secret reserve is mani-fold. It may be created for the purpose of equalizing dividends, or for profit. Lag funds to meet heavy losses without disclosing the fact to the general public, or for avoiding the disclosure of information to trade rivals.

Secret reserves are created in several ways:

- By under-valuation of stock-in-trade
- By making excessive provision for outstanding liabilities
- By over-depreciation of assets
- By charging capital items to revenue.

Since these operations either reduce the book value of the assets or increase the book value of liabilities without the fact being disclosed in the balance sheet, they become 'secret'. Hence they are called 'secret reserve'.

The auditors duty — the auditors position as regard 'secret reserve' is a difficult one. theoretically, there is no justification for creating one. Theoretically there is no justification for creating secret reserve because, then the balance sheet cannot show a true and correct view of the state of affairs of the concern. But in the case of large undertaking particularly in the case of banks, secret reserves are common and in practice, they are seldom referred to by the auditors in their reports.

Whether the auditor should refer to the existence of a secret reserve in his report or not depends on the circumstances of the particular case. The auditor should ascertain the amount of the reserve and the purposes for which it has been created. He should also study whether there is any chance for misusing it if the auditor is satisfied that secret reserve is necessary in the interest of the business, he need not deal with the matter in his report. If, however, he need not deal with the matter in his used for most improper purposes, he should not fail to refer the matter in his report, whatever may be the consequences on his personal interest, the auditor should endeavour to protect he interest of the shareholders.

Capital Reserve: Capital reserve is a reserve represented by capital items and not available for free distribution amongst the shareholders. It is created out of capital profits, such as surplus upon a revaluation of fixed assets, profits realized upon the sale of a fixed asset at a higher price than its book value, premium on an issue of shares or debentures, profit earned in purchasing a business at a price less than the value of its net asserts, etc. Capital reserve strengthens the financial position of the concern. It is ordinarily used for meeting capital losses, if any.

The Auditor should see that capital reserves represented by actual capital items and that it is shown distinctly in the Balance Sheet.

Revenue Reserve: Revenue reserve has been defined as 'any reserve other than a capital reserve'. It represents all amounts set a side which are free for distribution through the profit and loss account, e.g., dividend equalization fund, undistributed profit carried to general reserve.

The Contingent Liabilities

The contingent liabilities are liabilities which have not yet arisen or accrued, but may arise in future on the happening of certain events. They may or may not involve payment of money. The following are some instances of contingent liabilities:

1. Liability on Bills Receivable discounted and not yet matured;
2. Liability for calls on partly paid-up shares;
3. Liability on pending litigation;
4. Liability under a contract of guarantee;
5. Liability for penalties under contract, etc.

The contingent liabilities are dealt with in two different ways. The one way is to simply mention the nature of the liability on the face of the Balance Sheet by way of a footnote. The second way is to create a Reserve for the purpose. Some contingent liabilities may be anticipated. But the exact amount of loss to be borne may not be ascertained beforehand. Such they are merely noted on the face of the Balance Sheet. In some cases, the happening of contingency may be anticipated and the probable amount of liability that would accrue can also be estimated. Such liability is treated according to the second method. Adequate reserve is created out of the profits and shown as a liability in the body of the Balance Sheet. For instance, suppose, the amount of Bills discounted but not yet matured at the date of a Balance sheet is $.1,000. Then, there is a contingent liability to the extent of $.1,000. In the case of discounting of bills, the customer is bound to pay the amount of the bills to the Banker, if they are not met by the acceptors on maturity. But it may not be known at the date of the balance sheet how many bills would be dishonoured. Therefore, a note should be made in the Balance Sheet stating that there is a contingent liability in respect of bills under discount amounting to $.1,000. Suppose, if it is anticipated that bills amounting to, say, $.500 would be dishonoured and that the loss to that extent would be incurred in future, a Reserve for that amount should be created.

Auditor's Duty

This is rather a difficult task since they do not, in general, appear in the books of accounts. Special examination of various books of accounts should be necessary to find out the contingent liabilities. For instance, the bill Register should be examined to find out the liabilities on bills discounted but not yet matured. The minute book should be perused to ascertain the liability on pending contract or guarantee. The suit file and legal charges account should be examined to find out the liabilities on pending suits and so on.

The Auditor should enquire in to such liabilities and see that adequate reserves are created for those liabilities where a loss it's anticipated and those other liabilities are disclosed in the Balance Sheet by way of a footnote. Where there is no contingent liability, it is better for the Auditor to get a certificate to that effect from a responsible officer of the concern.

Self-learning Activity

Try to answer the following questions on your own:

1. How could you discover misappropriations of cash received from debtors?
2. How would you adjust the following items at the time of preparing final account?
   (*a*) Outstanding liabilities;
   (*b*) Outstanding assets, and
   (*c*) Pre-paid expenses

3. How would you audit deferred revenue expenditure?
4. Would you consider the following types of expenditure chargeable to capital or revenue?
   (*a*) Development expenditure
   (*b*) Special abnormally heavy advertising expenditure.
5. What are the depreciation methods?
6. As an auditor, what is your duty regarding depreciation?
7. Explain the Annuity Method.
8. How does sinking fund differ from an ordinary reserve fund?
9. What is the duty of an auditor as regards
   (*a*) General reserve;
   (*b*) Specific reserve?
10. What do you understand by capital reserve and revenue reserve?
11. What are contingent liabilities? How are they treated in the accounts?
12. What is the duty of an auditor as regards contingent liabilities?

Summary

- The auditor should adopt appropriate method for depreciation.
- Auditor duty as regards reserves, especially regarding specific reserves, he should consider the adequacy of reserves.
- Special examination of various books of accounts should be necessary to find out the contingent liabilities.

11 Verification and Valuation of Assets and Liabilities

Verification of Assets

After vouching various books of account, the Auditor has to turn his attention to the most important stage of his work, viz., the verification of assets. The verification of assets is considered to be his most responsible and onerous duty. If vouching is necessary to ascertain the correctness of transactions, the verification of assets is necessary to find out the truth of the balance sheet. The verification of assets means an examination of such evidences as will satisfy the Auditor that all those assets, which ought to exist at the date of the balance sheet, were actually in existence on that date.

The auditor's duty with regard to this matter is four-fold:

- *Firstly*, he should ascertain what assets ought to exist at the date of the balance sheet. The entries in the books of accounts (provided they are correctly recorded) will disclose the assets, which ought to be in the possession of the concern;
- *Secondly*, the auditor must verify, by actual inspection or otherwise, that such assets have existed actually at the date of the balance sheet;
- *Thirdly*, he should see that all the assets appeared at their proper values;

- *Lastly*, he should ascertain that all assets were free from any charges other than those disclosed in the books.

Valuation of Assets and Liabilities

The valuation of assets is an important matter in the preparation of the final account. The correctness of the profit and loss account and Balance sheet mainly depends on the proper valuation of assets and liabilities. The figures of net profit and loss and the balance sheet would be mere dead letters, if they were not based on proper valuation of assets. Any improper valuation may result in inflation of profits or falsification of accounts. The valuation of liabilities is an essay matter. As a rule, it is possible to ascertain the amounts of the liabilities exactly except in the case of contingent liabilities. But the difficulty is with the valuation of contingent liabilities. But the difficulty is with the valuation of assets. It is easy to find out the existence of assets, but difficult to value them correctly.

The question of valuation of assets is, in general a matter of estimation and personal opinion, but not of precision and absolute exactitude. The correctness of a valuation depends on the technical knowledge and experience of the valuer. The valuation life, etc. many of these factors are not susceptible for prelist calculation and estimation. Hence the difficulty of the precise valuation.

In practice, assets are valued according to certain conventional principles. Two bases are adopted in this respect. Certain assets are valued on the basis of market value or realizable value. Some are valued on the basis of their use-value to the business as a going concern. There is also another basis, viz., replacement value. It is the amount that would be required to purchase similar new asset, when the existing one becomes useless. What basis is to be adopted in a particular case is decided with reference to the nature of the asset, the purpose for which it has been acquired, its original cost, its working life, break-up value and the changes of it becoming obsolete. Valuation is made on the assumption that the business will not be closed, but will go on. The object of valuation is to make the balance sheet represent a fair and true view of the state of affairs of the concern.

Valuation of Fixed Assets

Fixed Assets are properties or possessions of a permanent nature. They are acquired by an undertaking for the purpose of using them in the business permanently for earning profits; they are not held for the purpose of sale. In short, fixed Assets are assets with which the business is carried on. For example, land and buildings and plant and machinery of a manufacturing concern are fixed assets. With the help of them, the activity is carried on.

The basis adopted for the valuation of fixed assets is their use-value. They are valued at historical or original cost price less any depreciation written off to the date. The value, then, represents the present worth of the assets to the business as a going concern. The amount of depreciation to be written off is estimated on the basis of the working life of the assets and their scrap-value, if any. The purpose of depreciation charge, according to the Association of certified and corporate Accountants, is not to provide for a fund for replacing the assets (this may be its incidental result) but for accounting as an expense the cost of using assets up. Depreciation is just designed to recover the prepaid cost of assets over their useful life. Neither the current realizable value nor the break-up value affects their working life therefore; such considerations are disregarded in estimating their value.

Thus Fixed Assets are valued according to their use-value to the business, i.e., their ability to serve the purpose for which they are acquired. They are not valued according to their intrinsic worth. In recent years, the purchasing power of money has gone down. With the result, fixed assets valued on the basis of historical cost appear in balance sheet as values far below their current. Scrap-value or break-up value is that amount that could be realized by selling an asset when it becomes unserviceable.

Replacement values: As depreciation is provided on such book values, amounts accumulated out of profits will be very inadequate. Considering these, it is sometimes suggested that fixed assets should be written up to their current values, crediting the surplus to capital reserve and providing depreciation on such appreciated values. This suggestion has not received the approval of the professional accountancy bodies. They recommend that until a practicable and acceptable alternative is available. Historical cost should continue to be the basis of valuation of fixed assets. But they have suggested a solution for solving the difficulties arising out of inflationary rise in prices. That is, when the difficulties arising out of inflationary rise in prices. That is, when the cost of replacing a fixed asset will be greatly in excess of its original cost, an additional amount could set aside to provide the further funds required for replacement. This additional amount would be credited to a special replacement provision account, while the usual depreciation calculated on historical cost would continue to be deducted from the book value of the asset in the Balance Sheet.

The Valuation of Floating (or) Circulating (or) Current Assets

Floating or circulating Assets are assets that are produced or acquired in the course of business. They are held for the purpose of sale. They are not held with a view to be used permanently, but merely for subsequent conversion into cash. Stock-in-trade, book debts and bills receivable are good instances of Floating or Circulating Assets.

They are floating on the current of business transactions. They pass through different stages of conversion and ultimately become cash. They are assets in which the trading is carried on; but not those with which it is conducted.

Since the floating Assets are held with a view to conversion into ready cash, they are valued on the basis of their realizable value (i.e., value-in-exchange). "Cost price or market price, whichever is lower" is the rule regarding the valuation of Floating Assets. When the market price is lower than the cost price, a loss is anticipated. Accordingly, the asset is valued at market price. On the other hand, the asset should not be valued above the cost price, simply because the market price is higher than the cost price. For if it is valued so, it would have the effect of taking into account a fictitious and unrealized profit.

To error on the safe side is wiser. In account-keeping, as a rule, provision should be made for anticipated losses, but anticipated profits should not be brought into account until they are actually realized. Under-estimation of profits, even if it is found to be incorrect at a subsequent date, will only be a benefit but seldom harm. But over-estimation of profits will certainly result in harm to the business, when it is found unjustified. Therefore, floating Assets should never be valued above cost price.

The Valuation of Wasting Assets

Wasting Assets are assets of a fixed nature, which are gradually consumed or exhausted in the course of the business, such as quarry and mine. Broadly speaking, Fixed assets like plant and machinery are also wasting assets, since their value is exhausted consequent upon wear and tear. However, there is one important difference between a wasting asset and a fixed asset. That is the amount of unexhausted portion of the wasting asset cannot be easily assessed, while the use-value of the fixed asset can be estimated at any time with a fair amount of accuracy.

The principle of valuation adopted for wasting Asset is more or less the same as that adopted for fixed assets. The value of exhausted or consumed portion is ascertained and the book value of the asset is reduced to that extent. In practice, the asset is allowed to remain in the books at the original value. And adequate amount of general reserve is created to cover up the depreciation.

Auditor's Duty

As regards the duty of an Auditor in connection with the valuation of assets, he need not be a valuer. The actual valuation is to be done by the management; the Auditor is concerned only with the correctness of the valuation. He should go through every detail. He should note the purpose for which the asset is acquired and study the method adopted for valuation. He should try to satisfy himself as regards the suitability of the method and the correctness of the calculations. He is required to ascertain that the valuation made appears to be fair and reasonable according to the accepted principles. He must make sure that no circulating asset is valued above the cost price on any account. He should also see that all anticipated losses have been provided for. An auditor is guilty of misfeasance, if he fails to detect the over-valuation is guilty of important assets like work-in progress when ample evidence is available for checking the accuracy of the figures given to him.

Stock-in-Trade (or) Inventories

Stock-in-trade is the unsold stock of goods on hand on the last day of a period. It should be brought into account and valued for the purpose of preparing the final account the result of trading is to be ascertained by means of preparing a Trading account for the period. If all the stocks are sold during the period itself, there is no question of valuation of closing stock at all. When there is some amount of unsold stock at the end of the period, it is to be assumed that the unsold stock is sold by the current year to the succeeding year. Only on that assumption the trading account is prepared with a credit for the value of closing stock. Stock in trade is brought in to account by debiting 'stock in trade account' and crediting the 'trading account' with the amount of its value, thus the value of stock in trade constitutes an important item of trading account therefore the correctness of the profit or loss depends, to a considerable extent on the accuracy of the valuation of the stock in trade. Hence the importance of the verification and valuation of this asset.

The extent of an Auditor's responsibility as regards the stock-in-trade is that, it is no part of the Auditor's duty to take stock and he is entitled to rely on other people for details of the closing stock. If he merely relies upon an official's certificate without checking or testing stock, the audit will be a mere force, for the accounts will show whatever results the official pleases.

Therefore the auditor should exercise reasonable care and skill with a view to satisfy himself as to the correctness of stock-taking and valuation. He should enquire into the whole system of stocktaking and the system of internal check with regard thereto, and satisfy himself as to the efficiency of the method. He should examine the stock-sheets, to make sure that the plant, loose tools, office furniture, etc., and goods held on consignment or on sale or return are excluded in the list. It has been suggested that the following steps should be taken by the Auditor while examining the stock-sheet:

1. Casting and a proportion of the calculations of major items in the stock-sheet should be checked.
2. The quantities shown in the book should be compared with the actual stock verified. Differences, if any, should be enquired in to.
3. Where stock is held by agents or in warehouses, certificates should be obtained and verified.
4. The entries in the Goods Inward Book for the last few days of the period should be examined in order to ascertain that the items brought into stock have been passed through the Bought Day Book and included in the purchases.
5. The Goods Outward Book should be examined and traced no item of sales was in the stock.
6. The basis of valuation should be enquired into. It should be seen that the stock is valued at cost or market price whichever is lower at the date of the Balance sheet and

that the value of the finished goods is below the market price. The items of obsolete or defective stocks should be valued at their respective realizable value.

7. The percentage of gross profit on turnover should be compared with that of the previous period and the causes of the marked fluctuations, if any, should be enquired into.

8. It should be seen that some responsible official has properly certified the stock- sheets, the parties concerned in the preparation having initialled them.

In this way, the auditor should satisfy himself that that the stock - in - trade taken into account was actually in existence at the date of the balance sheet and that the valuation of the same was made properly consistent with the accepted principles.

The most important point to be considered by the auditor this matter is to ascertain whether the same basis is adapted from year to year. If consistent basis were not so adopted, the trading results shown by the accounts would become distorted. The Auditor will do well if he states in his report the extent to which he relied on the certificate of the management. Any matter, which is not up to his satisfaction, should be dealt within his report.

Self-learning Activity

Try to answer the following questions on your own:

1. What is meant by 'verification of assets'?
2. How does verification differ from vouching?
3. State how would you verify the following:
   (*a*) Cash on hand;
   (*b*) Investments;
   (*c*) Freehold property; and
   (*d*) Goodwill

4. How would you verify and value:
    1. Machinery;
    2. Loose tools;
    3. Patents; and
    4. Bills Receivable?
5. What is the importance of valuation of assets?
6. Explain the principle adopted for valuation of floating assets.
7. What is auditor's duty as regards valuation of assets?

Summary

- The auditor should verify and value the assets with evidences thereof by following certain appropriate methods of valuation.
- By following the programme for final accounts audit and balance sheet audit he should examine the final accounts and balance sheet.

12 Audit Report

Form and Content

Audit Report

Reporting is essential to the audit process because it explains what the auditor did and the conclusions reached. Frequently, it is the only part of the audit users see. Therefore, from the users' point of view, the report is the auditor's product.

The basic requirements for issuing audit reports are derived from the four generally accepted auditing standards for reporting. The last standard is especially important because it requires an expression of opinion about the overall financial statements or a specific statement that an overall opinion is not possible, along with the reasons for not expressing an opinion. The standard also requires a clear-cut statement by the auditor of the nature of the examination and the degree to which the auditor limits his or her responsibility. Approximately half of the SASs involves reporting requirements.

The audit report is the final step in the entire audit process. The reason for studying it now, is to permit reference to different types of audit reports. The various types of audit report will be discussed in the next section elaborately. Now we know about the meaning and definition of audit.

Definition of Audit Report

According to Joseph Lancaster, "a report is a set of collected and considered facts, so drawn up as to give clear and concise information to persons who are not already in possession of the full facts of the subject matter of the report".

J.C.Ray defines audit report as, "the report shall either contain an expression of opinion regarding financial statements taken as a whole, or an assertion to the effect that an opinion cannot be expressed, when an overall opinion cannot be expressed, the reasons therefore should be stated. In all cases where an auditor's name is associated with financial statements the report should contain a clear cut indication of the auditor's examination if any, and the degree of responsibility he is taking".

So, we can mean an audit report is a letter communicating what was audited, management's and the auditor's responsibilities, what an audit entails, and the auditor's opinion. Most financial statements audits result in a three-paragraph standard audit report.

Parts of an Audit Report

The following discussion would make you clear about the parts of an audit report.

Regardless of the auditor, the following seven parts of the audit report remain the same. These parts are discussed hereunder:

1. *Report Title:* Auditing standards require that the report be titled and that the title include the word independent. For example, appropriate titles would be: 'independent auditor's report', 'report of independent auditor', or 'independent accountant's opinion'. The requirement that the title include the word 'independent' is intended to convey to users that the audit was unbiased in all aspects of the engagement.

2. *Audit Report Address:* The report is usually addressed to the company, its stockholders, or the board of directors. In recent years, it has become customary to address the report to the shareholders, to indicate that the auditor is independent of the company and the board of directors.

3. *Introductory paragraph:* The first paragraph of the report does three things: *First*, it makes the simple statement that the CPA firm has done an audit. This is intended to distinguish the report from a compilation or review report. The scope paragraph clarifies what is meant by an audit. *Second*, it lists the financial statements that were audited, including the balance sheet dates and the accounting periods for the income statement and statement of cash flows. The wording of the financial statements in the report should be identical to those used by management on the financial statements. *Third*, the introductory paragraph states that the statements are the responsibility of management and that the auditor's responsibility is to express an opinion on the statements based on an audit. The purpose of these statements is to communicate that management is responsible for selecting the appropriate generally accepted accounting principles and making the measurement decisions and disclosures in applying those principles, and to clarify the respective roles of management and the auditor.

4. *Scope paragraph:* The scope paragraph is a factual statement about what the auditor did in the audit. This paragraph first states that the auditor followed generally accepted auditing standards. The remainder briefly describes important aspects of an audit. The scope paragraph states that the audit is designed to obtain reasonable assurance about whether the statements are free of material misstatement. The remainder of the scope paragraph discusses the audit evidence accumulated and states that the auditor believes the evidence accumulated was appropriate for the circumstances to express the opinion presented.

5. *Opinion paragraph:* The final paragraph states the auditor's conclusions based on the results of the audit examination. This part is so important that frequently the entire report is referred to simply as the auditor's opinion. The opinion paragraph is directly related to the first and fourth generally accepted auditing standards.
6. *Name of the CPA firm:* The name identifies the CPA firm or practitioner that has performed the audit. Typically the firm's name is used, since the entire CPA firm has the legal and professional responsibility to make certain the quality of the audit meets professional standards.
7. *Audit Report date:* The appropriate date for the report is the one on which the auditor has completed the most important auditing procedures in the field. This date is important to users because it indicates the last day of the auditor's responsibility for the review of significant events that occurred after the date of the financial statements.

Auditor's Opinion

The profession of audit recognizes the need for uniformity in reporting as a means of avoiding confusion. Users would have considerable difficulty interpreting the meaning of an auditor's report if each were an original creation. The professional standards, therefore, defined and enumerated the types of audit reports that should be included with financial statements. The wording of audit reports is reasonably uniform, but different audit reports are appropriate for different circumstances.

The auditor expresses his opinion in the audit report after the audit process is completed. Based on the inquiry, interview, inspection, observation, reperformance and other techniques used by the auditor, he can have the idea about the performance, defects of the company. The auditor can express his opinion based on the check and tests conducted during the audit work.

Types of Auditor's Opinion

The auditor's opinion can be classified into four basic types: unqualified opinion, qualified opinion, adverse opinion, and disclaimer of opinion. Now we can have a look and understanding on each of the type of opinion.

Unqualified Opinion: A standard audit report given an unqualified opinion, which means it is the independent management's assertions (in an attestation) or financial statements (in an audit) are presented fairly in all material respects the financial position, results of operations, and cash flows in conformity with generally accepted accounting principles. To issue an unqualified opinion, the auditor must comply with generally accepted auditing standards. An unqualified opinion relates only to an entity's financial statements, not to the quality of the entity as an investment or credit risk.

Qualified Opinion: A qualified opinion means that except for the effects of a matter, management's financial statements present fairly in all material respects financial position, results of operations, and cash flows in conformity with generally accepted accounting principles. Only the term except for or same variation — such as except, exception, or with the exception of — may be used to qualify an opinion. Qualified opinions are issued when:

1. financial statements depart materially from generally accepted accounting principles;
2. management is unable to justify a material change in accounting principles; or
3. the scope of an audit is limited materially.

Adverse Opinion: An adverse opinion means management's financial statements do not present fairly in all material respects financial position, results of operations, and cash flows in conformity with generally accepted accounting principles. Adverse opinions are issued when:

1. financial statements depart from generally accepted accounting principles; or
2. management is unable to justify an account change, and the effect of the departure or change is so highly material that a qualified opinion is unwarranted.

Disclaimer of Opinion: A disclaimer of opinion means an auditor does not express an opinion on the financial statements. Generally, disclaimers are issued when:

1. the effects of scope limitation are so highly material that the auditor does not have a reasonable basis to an opinion; or
2. the auditor is not independent of management.

Self-learning Activity

Try to answer the following questions on your own:

1. Define audit report.
2. Point out the parts of an audit report.
3. What do you mean by auditor's opinion? Discuss adverse and disclaimer of opinion.

Summary

- The audit report is the final step in the entire audit process. an audit report is a letter communicating what was audited, management's and the auditor's responsibilities, what an audit entails, and the auditor's opinion. Most financial statements audits result in a three-paragraph standard audit report.
- There are seven parts in an audit report, which deals with the form and content of the audit report: report title, audit report address, introductory paragraph, scope paragraph, opinion paragraph, name of the CPA firm and audit report date.
- Auditor has to express his opinion after the completion of the audit work. The auditor's opinion can be: unqualified opinion, qualified opinion, adverse opinion and disclaimer of opinion.

Part — II

Cooperative Audit

13 Cooperative Audit

Cooperative Audit — Meaning, Definition, Objectives and Need

Cooperative Audit — Meaning

It is generally thought that the audit of a cooperative society is in no way different from that of a joint stock company. This idea is not correct. The purpose of a joint stock company is different profits making concern, while the latter is a service concern. The main object of the audit of a company of a partnership firm or and other profit seeding concern is simply to ascertain the correct net profits for a period. The audit of such concerns is merely a financial audit. That is, only the financial aspect of the transactions is checked. Transactions are carried on they are entered in the books in terms of money value. The result of such transactions is also measured in terms of money value. The entries are verified by the auditor to see whether they reflect the actual transactions in terms of money value and the correctness of the profit and the financial position are ascertained in relation to money value nothing more is done. Thus this audit is mainly a financial audit.

The audit of a cooperative society is different from this kind of audit. It is not a mere financial audit. It is not a mere examination of accounts to ascertain the correctness of financial aspect of the transactions. It is something more than this what is this 'something'? Let us examine. Why transactions are carried on? They are carried on to fulfill the object of the concern. In a profit making concern like a joint stock company transactions are transacted simply for the purpose of earning profits — to enhance the monetary value of the business. The transactions are not directly connected with the socio economic conditions of the shareholders of the concern. On the other hand, in a cooperative society, transactions are carried on not for their monetary aspect but for the sake of satisfying the needs of the members. The purpose of a cooperative society is not to earn profits, but to promote the economic welfare of its members. For this purpose only, the society enters in to transactions. As such the mere money value of transactions is not the primary factors. What is more important is the real effect of the transactions i.e., the extents to which they were useful in satisfying the economic needs of the members so as to promote their economic well-being let us explain this by an illustration. A member of a credit seeds to commence the showing in the proper time applied for a loan. Let us suppose that the loan was granted after the sowing period was over. Now, there was no use of such loan. Had it been granted in the proper time it might have been of real use to the borrower. Now there might be valid voucher for the disbursement of the 'delayed' loan. There might be proper sanction. It might have been properly recorded in the books from the point of an ordinary audit, the transactions is correct because it is supported by a valid evidence, properly sanctioned and correctly recorded. But what about its real effect? It did not serve the purpose for which it was intended. Therefore the object of examination of accounts of a cooperative society is not simply to ascertain the correctness of financial aspect of the transactions, but also to know their impact on the conditions of the members.

An audit of a cooperative society cannot and could not be a mere examination of bloods of account. Books of accounts after all they could serve the purpose of a rubber stamp. When a transaction is recorded in a book of account, it is expected that the entry in the book would reflect the transactions as it was. The auditor examines the entry to see whether it does so. But what aspect of the transaction is reflected by the entry? An entry is after all a mirror or a photograph. A mirror reflects only the outward appearance of a person before it. Can it reflect his internal qualities? It cannot. Similarly, a photograph shows the outward appearance of a person. It cannot reflect the character of intelligence of person. Such is the case with an entry in a book of account. However correct it may be it can only reflect the monetary aspect of the transactions for which it stands. It cannot mirror out neither the inner significances nor the real effect of the transaction. Therefore the cooperative auditors should not confine him to the books only. Of course he should not confine himself to the books only. Of course he should examine the entries in the books, ascertain their correctness and satisfy himself that they reflect the real transactions for which they stand. But they should not stop with that. That is only a first step. He should go further to reach the destination. He should go behind the books. He should make an enquiry in to the affairs of the society. He should explore the circumstances behind, if he should study its inner significance. He should examine the bearing of its effect on the purpose for which the society has been established. And see, on the whole, whether the transactions carried on by he society have received their purpose in fulfilling its object so as it enhance the economic welfare of its members.

Cooperative Audit — Definition

Cooperative audit may therefore be defined as an examination of accounts and an enquiry in to the affairs of the society in order to asserting the correctness of accounts and the extent to which the actives of the society were useful in promoting he socio-economic welfare of its members through the satisfaction of their needs in accordance with the principles of cooperation. Cooperative audit is thus something more than a mere financial audit. That is, it is also an administrative audit. — Dr. O.R. Krishnasawmi.

It "should embrace an enquiry in to all the circumstances which determine the general position of a society 'and aim at seeing' that the society is working on sound lines and the committee, the officers ands the ordinary members understand their duties and responsibilities.

According to Mirdha Committee on Cooperation, "audit should also embrace a scrutiny as to what extent the benefits of a society have accrued to the weaker or smaller among its members".

Objectives of Cooperative Audit

The objectives of cooperative audit are:

- To ascertain the correctness of accounts and records maintained by the cooperative enterprise;
- To ascertain the actual financial conditions and earning of the cooperative society;
- To detect and prevent the occurrence of errors and frauds;
- To assess how far the cooperative society has been able to carry on business on sound cooperative lines and secure economic benefit to its members; and
- To examine whether the affairs of the society have been carried on in accordance with the principles of cooperation and the provisions of cooperative law.

The examination and enquiries detailed above may be a tedious and difficult task but it must be done if the cooperative audit is to serve its real purpose. Those who feel that it is difficult to do this onerous tasked should console themselves with the saying of the ancient Greeks that " is not the easy things but the difficult things that are beautiful".

Need for Cooperative Audit

Cooperative audit is important and is needed in the following respects:

Protection of Members

The representatives from among the members are expected to carry on the administration of the society in accordance with the principles of cooperation. For this purpose they have to institute a check system over them. Audit is such check on the representatives in the interest of members. It enables the members to ascertain whether representatives have managed the society properly for the common interest of all. Thus audit is necessary for ensuring the proper management of the society.

Protection of Creditors

Audit is needed to know the credit worthiness of cooperatives. The creditors know the credit worthiness only through audit reports and financial statements published by the cooperatives. From this point of view also, cooperative auditing becomes essential.

Protection of Investors

Cooperatives accept deposits from the public. The depositors attach much importance to the audit of accounts of the societies. Audit gives them much confidence in the management of the societies and protects their interest by making the actual state of the affairs of the societies known.

Prevention of Frauds

Again big cooperative societies employ a number of paid servants to maintain their accounts and to carry on their affairs such employees are to be kept under constant vigilance. They are to be guarded against irregularity of work and commitment of frauds. An efficient audit provides such vigilance. It act as a check on the employees, makes them to be regular and efficient in their work and prevents the occurrence of errors and frauds as far as possible. Thus an audit is also required in order to promote efficiency and honesty among the employees of a cooperative society.

Successful Management

The cooperatives are chiefly composed of uneducated members. So that danger of their perversion to wrong ends is no means less besides, they use funds raised for weaker section consisting of small farmers, artisans and wage earners, and the handing of money involves certain temptations. These factors call for certain precautions. Auditing is one of such precautions to ensure successful management. Nothing is more important than a constant and vigilant secreting of the accounts and examines a precaution against mismanagements and failure.

Maintenance of the Public Image

In a country like Ethiopia where state patronage is extended to cooperatives on a substantial scale "audit is necessary to maintain the public image of co-operation and to assure the state and the general public that the movement is proceeding on right lines."

Self-learning Activity

Try to answer the following Questions on your own:

1. Define cooperative audit.
2. Why cooperative audit?

Summary

- Cooperative Audit is the application of general audit principles in cooperatives and it is more than an audit of company.
- Apart from the general objectives, cooperative audit has the objective of examining whether the affairs of the society have been carried on in accordance with the principles of cooperation and the provisions of cooperative law.

14 The Aspects of Cooperative Audit

There are two main aspects of cooperative audit. In the first place cooperative audit of a statutory audit. In the second place it is a state controlled audit. The first aspect is inevitable and common to audits of all concerns, which are managed by a few representatives on behalf of many proprietors. For instance, the audit of a joint stock company of a public utility concern is a statutory audit. However, the second aspect is not inherent in the system of cooperative audit in developing countries. It is necessitate the adoption of the system of state controlled audit in the cooperative movement. These two aspects are discussed hereunder in detail.

Cooperative Audit — A Statutory Audit

When the audit of a concern is compulsory under a statue, it is said to be a statutory audit. The audit of a cooperative society is compulsory according to an Act. According to the cooperatives societies proclamation every society shall be audited at least once in a year. Thus the audit of a cooperative society as explained earlier, if an association of a number of persons and it is managed by a few representatives on behalf of all the members. Their interest is to be safeguarded and looked after. The best means of protecting their interest is to institute a regular system of audit in order to check the accounts submitted by the representatives. But what is the guarantee that the accounts would be regularly audited at periodical intervals? Therefore, it becomes necessary to make it a legal obligation to have the accounts of the societies audited regularly. Thus the audit of co-operative societies has been made a statutory obligation. Moreover, cooperatives are public concerns. They deal with a large number of persons. Their activities are connected with the public at large. The proper management of the co-operatives, thus, becomes a matter of public importance. Proper management can be ensured through an efficient system of audit. Hence co-operative Audit is a *Statutory Audit*.

Co-operative Audit —A State-controlled Audit

The audit of a co-operative society in Ethiopia is not only a Statutory Audit, but also a State-controlled Audit. The state takes the initiative in arranging for the audit of societies registered under the co-operative Societies' Act. It directs and controls the system of Cooperative Audit through its co-operative officers, and market it a function of its own. The State assumes full responsibility for the audit of the accounts of the societies. The auditors of the co-operative societies are appointed or nominated by the State. They audit the accounts and submit their reports to the State. Co-operative Audit is, therefore, said to be a State-controlled Audit.

The co-operative Movement in developing has not been sponsored by the people themselves on their own accord. It is not a spontaneous movement. It is a movement sponsored by the Government in the interest of the common people. Since the Government took the main initiative in introducing the movement, it is naturally interested in its successful working also. The success of the movement depends on the proper management of the societies. But the societies deal mainly with masses that cannot boast of much education or organization. There are greater chances of the societies being mismanaged by unscrupulous self-interested parties, unless there is a strong control over their helm of affairs. Hence the control of societies becomes a great factor to be counted.

Proper control is necessary to avoid the pitfalls of mismanagement. Right guidance is essential for the progress of the movement on sound lines.

The answer is 'No'. The management of all societies by the government is neither feasible nor desirable. It is not feasible, because the vast structure of the movement is too unwieldy to be managed by single agency. It is undesirable, because external management is against the principle of co-operation. Co-operation. Co-operative societies are voluntary associations based on democratic principles. As such the members themselves should manage them.

It is a double-edged problem. On the one side, there is the necessity of having some control over the societies. On the other side, there is need for preservation of the principle of self-management. Audit solves this problem. It provides a 'control'. And at the same time it preserves the principle of societies. The information derived from the audit acts as a valuable guidance in developing the societies on proper lines. Again, the audit is a direct means for securing full information about their working which is necessary to study the progress of the movement. At the same time, the audit does not, in any way, infringe the rights of the members in managing their societies democratically. Accordingly the government has assumed the responsibility for audit of societies and it controls the whole system of Co-operative Audit through the Co-operative Departmental staff. Thus, State-controlled Audit is indispensable for co-operatives under the existing conditions in developing countries.

State Audit does not mean an audit at the cost of the government. It is not and need not be wholly state-paid audit. In the case of societies, which are in a position to bear the cost, the cost of audit is recovered from them by way of a levy of audit fees. In other cases the audit is done at the cost of the Government.

State Audit is only an environmental necessity. It is not an outcome of any structural phenomenon. It is rather contrary to the democratic nature of co-operative societies. It is just a transitory measure. it is needed only when the movement is not yet developed into a people's movement and needs outside control as a precaution against its perversion to wrong ends. When the movement begins to stand on its own legs and when the members of the societies become conscious of their rights and responsibilities so as to manage them on sound co-operative lines, there would be no longer any need for state control or audit. As rightly pointed out by Sheila Gorst, "When the co-operative movement develops and expands, it does not appear a suitable function for government to maintain permanently a large staff of cooperative auditors".

The need for State-controlled audit arises chiefly in underdeveloped countries like India, Pakistan and African countries. is these countries, the co-operative movement did not originate spontaneously as a people's movement, but has been sponsored by the Government. Hence in such countries, the government with a view to see whether societies are managed on sound lines, get their accounts audited through its departmental staff or authorized auditors. Such state audit is necessary only till the movement develops into a people's movement. There is no need for State-controlled audit when the movement originates spontaneously as a people's movement. Then members themselves will take care of the proper management and success of their societies this is true in the case of British, Danish, Swedish and Central European Co-operative Movements. In these countries Co-operative audit is not a State-controlled audit. in England the accounts of affiliated consumers societies are audited by the audit department of the wholesale society. In central Europe, special organizations, viz., and regional unions carry on audit. Is Sweden, the Federation of Unions audits the accounts of farmer's co-operatives? In Italy, national co-operative unions do audit.

Even in underdeveloped countries, state audit of co-operatives need not be a permanent feature. It should be gradually replaced by a system of non-official audit; for, co-operatives, being democratic institutions, should manage themselves all their affairs, including audit. But each society cannot get its accounts audited by its own staff. Such an arrangement cannot be an audit, as audit is an examination of accounts done by an independent agency. Then how co-operatives could do this by adopting the principle of federalism. Just as they federate for purposes of finance and education and organize central financing agencies and co-operative unions respectively, they can set up a federal organization of their own for audit also. That is, they can organize audit unions. These unions can maintain qualified audit staff and through them audit the accounts of member-societies. Alternatively central financing agencies or co-operative unions may also undertake auditing of member-societies. Thus the co-operative movement itself could make its own arrangement for the audit of the co-operatives. This should be the ultimate pattern. However, the Government, for the sake of giving confidence to the members of co-operatives, could retain responsibility for certifying that staff appointed was capable of undertaking audits. It could also retain the right to conduct test or 'surprise' audit so as to ensure that unions audit the accounts of societies efficiently and promptly.

An ideal system of audit implies a combination of concurrent and final audits, the former being done by one agency and the latter by another. From point of view of efficiency, the system of co-operative audit seems to serve the purpose of an ideal audit. it is because that both concurrent and final audits are carried on in co-operative societies in some form or another. The final audit of a society is done by an independent agency, viz., the Government. It is the statutory duty of the Registrar through audit wing to cause every registered society to be audited at least once in a year. He carries on this duty through the departmental staff or authorized auditors.

Self-learning Activity

Try to answer the following questions on your own:

1. Why State controlled audit is necessary in cooperatives?
2. What should be the ultimate system of audit in cooperatives?

Summary

- There are two aspects: 1. Statutory audit; and 2. State-controlled audit. The various kinds of cooperative audits are: 1. interim, 2. concurrent; 3. final; and 4. test audit.
- There are points of differences in terms of statutory obligation, qualification of an auditor, etc., between cooperative audit and company audit.

15 Kinds of Cooperative Audit

The different kinds of cooperative audit in force at present are therefore four in numbers. They are:

1. interim audit;
2. concurrent audit;
3. final audit; and
4. test audit.

It must be pointed out that these four kinds of audit are not mutually exclusive: but they are complimentary to one another.

Interim Audit

Interim audit is nothing but a concurrent system of audit as applied to the audit of certain types of societies such as rural cooperative credit societies. It is conducted in the interim period between one final audit and the other. Ordinarily, the interim audit is taken up from December or January and competed by the end of June. During the interim audit, the auditor checks the financial transactions form the date of the previous final audit to the date of his visit and verify ledger balances. A statement of receipts and disbursements for the period is prepared; administrative check is done in great detail. It involves a detailed investigation in to the affairs of the society. It includes a more detailed enquiry in the light of principles of cooperation and with reference to the act, rules and by laws verification of loans and examination of the items in the property statement of members are carried on extensively. A detailed list of defects noticed is also prepared. The auditor s memorandum is prepared in duplicate in the prescribed printed from. The auditor gives the original to the society. The duplicate is submitted to the office of the district cooperative audit officer along with the copies of the schedule of defects.

Interim audit minimize the work of the final audit to a great extent with respect to mechanical checking and administrative investigation. It enables the auditor to get through the final audit quickly, to detect and prevent errors early and to give the society a view of its working at least once in six months. The junior auditors do interim audit.

Concurrent (or) Running (or) Continuous Audit

Concurrent audit is one which is done during the course of the period under review, the auditor being engaged continuously throughout the year or in the alternative attending to his work at frequent intervals or at least once in a quarter during the period it is an audit done during the cores of the year under review. It is not an audit commenced after the end of the period. Hence the term 'concurrent audit'. For instance, if the accounts of a society for the period from July 1, 1998 to June 30,1999 are audited at any time between July 1,1998 to June 30, 1999, then it is said to be concurrent audit.

This kind of audit is adopted in big societies like central and urban banks cooperative central stores, sugar mills, spinning mills etc. where the work involved is considerable and where it would be disadvantageous to commence the audit after the end of the period. These societies generally take the services of auditors exclusively for their audit and bear their cost. Concurrent audit is done purely by the departmental staff it is mainly a mechanical audit and no special printed from is prescribed to submit a report after it is conducted.

However concurrent audit reports may be submitted in the following form:

> Concurrent audit report for the month of ....199...
>
> 1. Name of the society
> 2. Date of audit
> 3. Period of audit
>
> Certified that:
>
> *(i)* The cash balance of $ ....at the close of business on......199...., was verified and found to agree with the balanced according to the day book;
>
> *(ii)* I checked the receipts and vouchers relating to the transactions in the period of audit and found them correct (except is pointed out in the schedule of defectors);
>
> *(iii)* The posting in all the ledgers including the general ledger have been checked and found correct; wrong and misprinting and other mistakes were got rectified then and there;
>
> *(iv)* The establishment and contingent charges incurred by the society are authorized and necessary and are in accordance with the budget approved by the general body;
>
> *(v)* The by laws have not been infringed (except in respect of instances pointed out in schedule of defects; and
>
> *(vi)* Ledger balances were verified and the totals of such balances agree with the figures noted in the general ledger.
>
> *Signature of Appropriate Authority*

Final Audit

Final audit is the statutory annual audit conducted in every registered society after the end of every year. It is a completed audit for the year, leading together closing of accounts for the year and the preparation of the receipts and payments statement the balance sheet and the profit and loss account. The work involved in the final audit consists of a mechanical check and administrative examination of the books of accounts etc., from the date up to which the interim or concurrent audit has been complete till the last date of the cooperative year. It also includes verification of cash balance and securities, valuation and verification of assets and liabilities and examination of overdue debts, if any with special reference to the statutory obligation under the act.

Final audit should be conducted in such a manner as to ascertain the extent to which the society was useful in improving the economic conditions of its members. There is no use of simply satisfying with the ascertainment of the financial portion of the society as reflected by the balance sheet a thorough investigation in to the affairs of the society should be made in order to gauge the benefit rendered by it to its members.

The final audit memorandum (i.e., report) is prepared in the prescribed form. The form varies according to the types of societies. It is submitted to the district audit officer with the various schedules such as the details of suspense assets and liabilities, details of non-statutory reserves, list of overdue debts lists of bad and doubtful debts, confirmations obtained from creditors and debtors and certificate of the board of directors regarding the assets of the society.

Schedules of defects are also submitted along with the audit memorandum. The particulars of contraventions of the act rules and the by laws of the society misappropriating of cash, material irregularities in the payments and other matters specified by the registrar are furnished in the schedules of defects. The auditors should also furnish the certificate in the prescribed form.

If the auditors discovers any material irregularity affecting the financial position of the society or violations of acts and rules or misappropriation of funds, he should submit a special reports to the district officer furnishing full particulars of such irregularities.

Test Audit

Test audit is an audit conducted in order to test the correctness of the final audit done by any auditory. It is an audit of the accounts of certain number of societies which an auditor has final authority. Test audit is out an examination of accounts at random. It is a full re-audit of all accounts of society. But all societies are not test audited during a year only a certain parentage of societies are test audited.

The need for a test audit—test audit is a peculiar feature of cooperative audit. The responsibility for the audit of accounts of the cooperative societies vests on the registrar. But it is humanly impossible for him to carry on the audit of all societies within his jurisdiction. So he delegates his power to the departmental staff consisting of senior and junior auditors naturally, he has to satisfy himself that this subordinates are doing their work properly. To test their work and efficiency, test audit is therefore needed.

The objects of test audit are:

1. to check the efficiency of audit staff;
2. to find out the mistakes committed by them so as to guide them to do their work properly; and
3. to ensure correct and efficient audit of societies.

The method of conducting test audit — test audit is conduced by the superior departmental officers like district audit officers. The officer in the presence of the auditor who conducted the final audit of the society conducts test audit.

At least one society of each auditor is to be test audited. Proper selection of societies is more important. Societies with sufficient transactions are to be selected. The list of selected societies should be representative and include a stores society a marketing society, a weavers society and agricultural bank, a marketing society etc. only such of the societies as were not test audited in the proceeding three years are to be selected for test audit during a year super audit.

Super Audit

The audit of societies should be first done by a staff maintained by cooperative institution themselves and latter by a government staff. It is termed as the audit to be done by the government staff as 'super audit'. The super audit is not a mere testing of a previous made at longer intervals than the original annual audit "the super audited once in every two years, but after a period of four of five years the interval might be enlarged to three years and perhaps still larger intervals might be permitted in the more distance future".

This system of super audit was later introduced in developing countries. But the system of non-official audit to supplement, which the super audit system was recommended, did not develop. Governments had to get the societies audited mainly by their departmental staff as the governmental staff was thus to conduct the original audit of societies super audit became redundant and unnecessary. Therefore it was abolished in 1933.

Self-learning Activity

Try to answer the following questions on your own:

1. Define and distinguish between:

(*a*) Continuous audit;

(*b*) Completed audit; and

(*c*) Test audit.

Summary

- There are four kinds of cooperative audit— interim, concurrent, final, and test audit. The super audit discussed in the chapter is abolished.

16 Difference Between Cooperative Audit and General Audit

Difference Between Cooperative Audit and Company Audit

The audit of accounts of a cooperative society is conducted as per the provisions of cooperative societies act. It is a state audit directed and controlled by the government through the Federal agency of cooperatives societies.

The audit of accounts of Joint Stock Company is regulated and governed by the portions of different sections of the Companies Act of the respective countries. It is an affair of the company itself. Both these audits are obligatory according to the statute governing each. That is the audit in both cases in a statutory function however; there are certain points of difference between them in methods and scope of work this difference may be enumerated as follows:

1. *Statutory obligation* — In a cooperative society the arrangement for audit is a statutory obligation placed on the registrar of cooperative societies. Hence it is not only a statutory audit but also a state controlled audit. On the other hand, the arrangement for audit of a joint stock company is an annual obligation vested on the company itself. As such it is a statutory audit only. And not a state controlled audit.
2. *The appointment of auditors* — The appointment of the auditor of company is made by general body of its share holders and in some cases by the board of directors. Thus

the appointment of the auditor is an affair of the company itself but in the case of a cooperative society, the members of the society are generally nothing to do with the appointment of the auditors. The registrar of cooperative societies appoints or authorizes 'some person' on his behalf to conduct the audit of the accounts of the society. Hence the appointment to the auditor is not the function of the society but affairs of the registrar.

3. *The purpose of appointment* — In a joint stock company, an auditor is appointed to act mainly as an agent of the shareholders to carry out an independent investigation in to its affairs and to report the results to them for their satisfactions. The auditor of a cooperative society on the other hand, has to assure the government that it is working and developing on sound lines 'in accordance with cooperative principles'.

4. *The object of audit* — The most important purposes of the audit of a company is to disclose the profit available for dividend and to ascertain the true and correct view of the state of affairs. But in a cooperative society which is a union of persons the primary object of the audit is to ascertain how far the society has been able to carry on its business on sound cooperative lines securing the ultimate object of material and moral improvements of its members.

5. *The administrative check* — The administrative check is a special feature of cooperative audit a part from the examining of financial aspect of the transactions, a detail enquiry in to the affairs of the society is conducted in order to ascertain that they have been conducted in accordance with the principles of cooperation and the provisions of the act, rules and by laws but the company audit is only a financial audit. The contrary aspect of the transactions is examined in order to ascertain the true financial potion of the concern. In a cooperative society,

an audit is not for audit sake, but for the sake of the assessment of the benefit rendered by the society to its members in relation to their economic welfare.

6. *The essential principle* — The essential principle of audit viz., the independence of the auditor is best provided for in the system of a cooperative audit. For, the cooperative auditor is not permitted to be a member of the society, the account of which he is auditing. He works under no obligation to the societies under his charge. But in the case of a company there is nothing to prevent it from appointing any one of its shareholders as its auditor, provided he possesses the required qualifications prescribed for the purpose.

7. *Preparation of final accounts* — The auditor of a company need not prepare the final accounts and balanced sheet, which he is to certify. He is not an accountant. He is there simply to examine the accounts already prepared by others, whereas in the case of a cooperative audit, the auditor himself prepares the final accountant the balance sheet of the society, which he is auditing.

8. *Calculation of interest* — In a cooperative society items of interest overdue and interest overdue and interest accrued the after the excluded from the net profit, simply because their reliability it doubtful. But in the case of a company which is essentially a profit seeking concern, much care is taken in ascertaining the profit an all out standing items of income including interest overdue and interest accrued their crafter are included in the profit.

9. *Scope of audit* — The audit of a cooperative society shall include an examination of overdue debts, if any the verification of the cash balances and securities and a valuation of the assets and liabilities of the society. On the other hand the auditor of company is not a value the valuation is made by the management his duty is merely; confined to asserting whether such valuation is reasonable.

10. *The rights and responsibilities of the auditor* — The rights of a cooperative auditor are wider; his duties and responsibilities are extensive and onerous. He shall have free access not only to books and accounts by also the cash securities and other properties in the possession of the society, he shall have the power to issue summons to the concerned persons to produce the books of the society, if they are refused to show to him. There is no such power in the case of an auditor of a company. Again a cooperative auditor has not only to verify the accounts but also to assess so far the society had fulfilled its mission. The duty of company auditors is merely to ascertain whether the balance sheet reflects a true and fair view of the affairs of the company.

11. *Disclosure of facts* — in a cooperative audit maximum possible publicity must necessarily be give to all items in the balance sheet. There is no need for concealing or bolstering up any matter in the balance Sheet. There is no question of 'secret reserve' or 'window pressing' which are often restored to in the balance sheet of a company.

Thus, the audit of a cooperative society is mere comprehensive and elaborate than that of a joint stock company while the latter is simply an examination of accounts and ascertainment of their accuracy, the former is something more than that. It is also an enquiry in to the affairs of the society which was helpful in improving the economic condition of its members and satisfaction of their common economic needs.

Rights, Duties and Responsibilities of Cooperative Auditor and Those of Company Auditors Compared

Rights and Powers Compared

According to the Companies Act, an auditor of a company shall have a right of access at all times to the books and accounts and vouchers of the company.

On the other hand an auditor of a cooperative society shall have free access not only to the books, accounts and documents but also to cash securities and other properties belonging to or in the custody of the society.

Secondly, an auditor of a company shall be entitled to require from the directors and officers of the company such information and expansion as the auditor may think necessary for the performance of his duties as an auditor.

But the corresponding power of a cooperative auditor is more elaborate. He is entitled to receive information regarding the transactions and working of the society from its officers but also from its members — past and present and employees.

Thirdly, the auditor of a company shall be entitled to receive notice of and to attend any general meeting and to be heard at any general meeting, which he attends on any part of the business, which concerns him as auditor.

Similar power has been conferred on the cooperative auditor in some countries as per the cooperative law.

Fourthly, a cooperative auditor may summon any person in possession or responsible for the custody of books, accounts and other properties to produce the same at any place at the headsquarters of the society or any branch thereof.

An auditor of a company has no such power. He needs no such power. For, he is acting on behalf of the shareholders of the company and it is their duty to make arrangements for placing necessary books and documents before the auditor.

Duties and Responsibilities Compared

In the first place, whereas an auditor of a company is required to made a report to the members of the company on the accounts and balance sheet examined by him. An auditor of a cooperative society being an agent of the government submits his report to the cooperative department.

Secondly, a company auditor is required to report whether or not he has obtained all the information and explanation required and whether or not the balance sheet and profit and loss account are drawn up in conformity with the law.

On the other hand a cooperative auditor in addition to this has to examine that all the affairs of the society were carried on in accordance with the principles of cooperative, the act, rules and by laws.

Thirdly the auditor of a company has to ascertain whiter the balance sheet exhibits a true and fair view of the company affairs.

But the duty of the auditor of a cooperative society does not confine with the mere examination of the balance sheet he should conduct a thorough investigation in to the affairs of the society so as to assess the extent of benefits rendered by the society to its members.

Fourthly, according to a legal decision it is not the duty of a company auditor to act as a value. But a cooperative auditor is required specifically to make valuing and verification of the assets (including cash balance and securities) and liabilities.

Fifthly, an auditor of a cooperative society is specially required to make an examination of overdue debts , if any but in the case of the auditor of a company , there is no such specific requirement .

Sixthly, while the auditor of a company , has to state whether in his opinion books of accounts have been kept by the company as required by the Companies Act, the cooperative auditor has to see that the society maintains all the books and register prescribed by the rules framed under the cooperative societies act.

Lastly, the auditor of a company is its agent to a certain extent, since he is acting on behalf of the shareholders but there is no such agential responsibility on the part of a cooperative auditor who is acting independent of the members and officers of the society.

From this comparative sketch, it is evident that the rights and powers of the cooperative auditor are wide and compressive and his duties are more onerous and responsible than those of the auditor of a company.

Self-learning Activity

Try to answer the following questions on your own:

1. Compare (*a*) the rights and powers; and (*b*) the duties and responsibilities of cooperative auditors with those of company auditors.
2. Try to list out the points of differences between cooperative audit and general audit.

Summary

- There are points of differences between cooperative audit and general audit. By seeing that cooperative audit is a social audit.

17 Cooperative Audit Programme

Preparation for Audit

An audit like an examination requires certain preparation before its commencement. Before coming the actual work auditing, the auditor should study certain points:

- *First* he should study the cooperative societies act and the rules and frames under it since cooperative audit is a statutory audit and it governed by the cooperative societies act. It is essential that the auditor should have a knowledge of the act for the purpose of ascertaining that the affairs of the society are carried in accordance with the act and rules.
- *Secondly,* he should ascertain what sort of audit — final of interim or concurrent audit — he is required to conduct. This as be ascertained by reference to the instruction received from the office of the district cooperative audit officer.
- *Thirdly,* he should make himself familiar with the nature of the business of the society and its technical details, if any for the purpose of easily understanding the meaning of various transactions of the society.
- *Fourthly,* he should study the by law of the society, with particular reference to its objects, its area of operation value of the share, the maximum number of share that a member can take the borrowing limit of the society and the person or persons authorized to receive and pay money.

- *Fifthly,* he should obtain a list of books maintained by the society and study the relation of one book to another. Perusal of the list of books are necessary in order to ascertain whether the society maintains all the books and registers prescribed under the rules framed under the act .
- *Sixthly,* he should ascertain the respective duties and responsibilities of the number of the staff, if any, and he scope of the authority of each members of the staff.
- *Seventhly,* he should study the method of account keeping adopted in the society and examine the method of arrangement of internal check or audit, if any, in vogue .
- *Eighthly,* he should make a perusal of the previous years audit report and the summary of defects in order to ascertain if the defects noted therein have been rectified.
- *Ninthly,* he should go through the minutes book of the society and make note of the resolutions relating to accounts.
- *Lastly,* he should make note of the instructions receive from the chief audit officer registrar in the form of circulars, orders or memorandums relating to the accounts and administration of the society.

Then he can chalk-out programme of work to perform it in a methodical way.

Audit Programme

Audit programme is a scheme of work and diary of work as well. It is indispensable for efficient audit. It set-outs in detail the different phases of the work to be done in the course of the audit. It should be so drawn that the entire work will be completed within the time allotted for. In the case of big societies whose audit is done by an auditor assisted by a number of junior auditors, the audit scheme pre plans and pre determines the work to be done by each, so as to ensure maximum efficiency and reasonable progress. Audit programme is useful of a guide for during schemes for the future also. The phases of work that are covered up are marked then and there in the programme. This will afford material for the revision of the audit programme on a realistic basis. While certain aspects of work such as examination of the by laws perusal of minute books and obtainment of a statement of internal check and a list of books are common to all types of cooperative certain other aspects according to the types of societies. The audit of every type of the society involves certain special features.

Certain model audit programme is given below. These may be adapted according to the scope, size and the nature of the business of the concerned societies.

Audit Programme (COMMON)

The phases of work which are common to all types of societies are:

1. Keep a note book for recording all important points which the auditor if finds during the course of audit.
2. Get himself conversant with the working of the society and the technical details of its business.
3. Study the by laws of the society and to note down the following particulars:
   - (*a*) The area of operations and the objects of the society;
   - (*b*) The value of a share;
   - (*c*) The maximum number of shares that a member can hold;
   - (*d*) The borrowing power of the society;
   - (*e*) The composition of the committee of management and its powers
   - (*f*) The person or persons authorized to receive money;
   - (*g*) The person responsible for the safe custody of and other properties of the society; and
   - (*h*) The mode of distribution of profits.

4. Obtain a list of books maintained by the society and study their mutual relationship.
5. Study the method of account keeping and the system of internal check in vogue.
6. Study the previous years audit memorandum and the schedules of defects and note down points which require examination of to be remembered in the course of audit.
7. Study the minutes book of the society and make note of the resolutions relating to accounts and administration.
8. Study the minutes book of the society and make note of the society and make note of the resolutions relating to accounts and administration.
9. Read the circulars, orders and memorandums received from the registrar and chief audit officer and note down the points relevant to the accounts and administration.
10. Verify the balance.
11. Open a register of defects to note down the defects then and there.
12. Vouch the cash book (or day book) and check the postings form the cash book in to the special ledgers and the general ledger.
13. Check the postings from the cash book into the special ledgers and the general ledger.
14. Check the totals of the ledger accounts and their balances.
15. Conduct administrative audit.
16. Prepare the statement of receipts and disbursements for the period.
17. Calculate the amounts of outstanding assets and liabilities as on the last date of the year and tabulate them in to a list.
18. Verify assets and liabilities.
19. Prepare the balance sheet as on the last date of the year.

20. Prepare the profit and loss account for the year.
21. Fill in audit memorandum.
22. Prepare the schedules of defects as prescribed in the rules
23. Submit the audit memorandum with all enclosures and the schedules of defects to the district level officer.

Audit Programme (SPECIAL ITEMS)

In addition to these common items of work, certain special items of work are involved in the audit of every type of society. They are listed hereunder:

Cooperative Credit Societies

The following are the items coming under the audit programme of credit societies:

1. Check the postings in to:
   (i) the annual credit statement prepared under crop loan system;
   (ii) the ledger of borrowings;
   (iii) loan ledger;
   (iv) liability register;
   (v) property statement of members in unlimited liability societies;
   (vi) register of fluid resource;
   (vii) register of closed loans; and
   (viii) register of movable properties.
2. Examine overdue debts an classification of loans under good, bad and doubtful.
3. Calculate interest accrued on loans due by members.
4. Verify items in property statement in the case of unlimited liability society.
5. Verify loans, (i.e.) to prepare a list of loans due by members and to get their signatures against their dues

by meeting them either in a meeting or individually and to verify as many of the receipts issued to the members as possible very jewels loans, if any and to physically verify all the jewels held by the society.

6. Verify jewel loans if any and to physically verify all the jewels held by the society.
7. Verify stock of produce, if any pledge as security for loans.
8. Verify bonds executed by member borrowers.
9. Examine whether any loan is time barred.
10. Check the accounts relating to any credit activities of the society such as supply of agricultural requirements and distribution of domestic goods.

Land Mortgage (Or Development) Bank

The following are the items coming under the audit programme of land mortgage bank.

Primarily land mortgage bank:

1. vouch loan applicant fees collected from applicants for investigation of their titles to lands offered as security and recoveries towards loans made under the equated instalment system or the fixed instalment system;
2. examine the adequacy of value of lands offered as security;
3. examine the titles of borrowers to lands offered security and their repaying capacity;
4. examine the actions taken against defaulters;
5. examine the executing of decrees made against defaulters and the sale of their lands.

Central land mortgage bank:

1. scrutinize the records relating to issue of debentures and examine the arrangements made for redeeming debentures;

2. scrutinize title deeds and mortgaged bonds executed by borrowers and their safe custody
3. examine the orders of the trustee as regards the disposal of recoveries made from primary banks and their implementing
4. verify the accounts relating to the debenture redemption fund and its investment
5. verify the securities in which the debenture redemption fund and the reserve fund have been invested.

Consumer Cooperative Stores

The following are the items coming under the audit programme of consumer cooperative stores.

1. Vouch purchases and expenses on purchases, examining of the procedure laid down by the committee or the by laws for purchases has been adhered to.
2. Study the double compartmental system in vogue.
3. Examine price fixation.
4. Vouch sales with reference to sale chits and daily sales book.
5. Check salesmen's indents book, registrar of issues of salesmen and sale means liability register.
6. Check posing in to the purchases, issue and stock register of trade deposits suppliers personal ledger members credit purchases register of bonus on purchases and register so empties.
7. Examine the stock depreciator and defect in stock.
8. Prepare trading account in addition to other usual final statements and account.
9. Make a critical study of the results of trading.
10. Examine how far the society was able to supply pure and unadulterated goods to the members at fair prices and without unreasonable delay.

Production and Sale Societies

The following are the items coming under the audit programme of production and sale societies.

1. Vouch purchases of raw materials
2. Vouch expenses on purchases
3. Vouch issue of raw materials to members
4. Vouch receipts of finished goods from members and the corresponding recoveries of materials from them
5. Vouch payment of advances to members
6. Vouch payment of wages and collection of thrifty deposits
7. Vouch sale of finished goods
8. Check sales classification
9. Vouch payment of bonus on wages
10. Check postings in to the following species registers:
    - *(i)* raw materials stock register;
    - *(ii)* raw material issue register;
    - *(iii)* job cards or appraisers tickets and finished goods receipts register;
    - *(iv)* wages register;
    - *(v)* thrift deposits register;
    - *(vi)* materials recovery register;
    - *(vii)* finished goods stock register;
    - *(viii)* personal ledger;
    - *(ix)* debtors ledger; and
    - *(x)* register of bonus on wages.

Marketing Societies

The following are the items coming under the audit programme of marketing societies:

1. Vouch receipt of produce for sale on commission basis.
2. Vouch outright purchases of produce.
3. Vouch sale of produce.
4. Vouch loans issued on the pledge of produce.
5. Vouch purchases and sales of fertilizers, etc.
6. Vouch payments of sale proceeds to members and recoveries of loans and other amounts due from members, under the scheme of integrated credit and marketing.
7. Vouch commission earned on agency business.
8. Vouch accounts relating to maintenance and use of lorries owned.
9. Check postings in to the following additional ledgers:
    (i) stock register for produce revived on agency basis;
    (ii) stock register of outright purchases and sales;
    (iii) auction register;
    (iv) stock registers of fertilizers, etc.;
    (v) loan ledger;
    (vi) members personal register; and
    (vii) register of bonus on sales.
10. Verify produce pledge and stock of owned produce.

Cooperative Processing Societies

The following are the items coming under the audit programme of processing societies:

1. Vouch purchases of raw materials and expenses on purchases.
2. Vouch maintenance expenses.
3. Vouch maintenance expenses.
4. Vouch costing register.

5. Vouch sale of processed good, and by products.
6. Check stock register for raw materials stock register for finished goods and stock register for by products.
7. Verify and value stocks of raw materials finished goods and by products.

Housing Societies

The following are the items coming under the audit programme of housing societies

1. Vouch site cost register.
2. Vouch government loan ledger.
3. Vouch issue of loans or cost of construction of houses.
4. Vouch purchase, issue and stock of building materials verify bonds and agreements executed by members.
5. Vouch recovery of installment from members.

Milk Supply Societies and Unions

The following are the items coming under the audit programme of milk societies

1. Vouch loans granted to members for purchases of milk animals.
2. Vouch repayment of loans by members in instalments.
3. Examine overdue debt if any.
4. Vouch purchases and sale of milk, and collecting of the proceeds from vendors.
5. Examine the agreements entered in to by members for regular supply of milk to the society and their strict observance a practice.
6. Check the accounts relating to collection of dues from the regular customers to whom milk is sold on credit.
7. Vouch payment of price of milk to members.

8. Check the accounts relating to conversion of surplus milk in to by products like palgova, butter, etc.
9. Check the accounts relating to maintenance of vans owned, if any for the transport of milk.
10. Check the trip sheets kept for the use of vans.
11. Check the accounts relating to supply of fodder animal feed etc, to members and the recovery of their cost of the amount payable to them towards the cost of milk supplied
12. Check disbursement of bonus to members out of net audits in proportion to the value of milk supplied.

Motor Transport Societies

The following are the items coming under the audit programme of motor transport societies:

1. Check daily collections of bus or lorry with references trip cards chaplains of remittance and collection register.
2. Check the accounts relating to collection of hire change by lorry drivers with reference to the temporary receipt books used by the drivers, trip sheets and the permanent receipt book maintained by the officer.
3. Check the accounts relating to cost of repairs and renewals.
4. Check the accounts relating to purchases, issued and maintenance of spare parts and tools.
5. Check the register of stock of spare parts and tools with the indents and log books of vehicles.
6. Check the accounts relating to the condemned and replaced parts.
7. Vouch consumption of petrol and oil with reference to trip-sheets, bills and accounts rendered by suppliers of petrol and oil and the standards regarding mileage per litre.

8. Check/vehicle wear income and expenditure
9. Verify the accounts relating to sale of condemned vehicles.

Cooperative Farming Societies

The following are the items coming under the audit programme of housing societies:

1. Check the accounts relating to land and other resources pooled by members.
2. Vouch loans and subsidies received from the government and their utilizing.
3. Check the expenditure incurred for the improvement of lands and its apportionment of different plots.
4. Vouch purchase and maintenance of livestock.
5. Vouch purchase and maintenance of implants pump sets, machinery, tools, etc.
6. Verify the accounts relating to the purchases and use of seeds, fertilizers, pesticides fodder etc.
7. Vouch consumption of petrol and oil with reference to trip sheets, bills and accounts rendered by supplies of petrol and oil and the standards regarding mileage per litre.
8. Check vehicle wear income and expenditure.
9. Verify the accounts relating to sale of condemned vehicles.

Cooperative Housing Societies

The following are the items coming under the audit programme of housing societies:

1. Check the accounts relating to land and other resources pooled by members
2. Vouch loans and subsidies received fro the government and their utilization
3. Check the expenditure incurred for the improvement of lands and its apportionment to different plots

4. Vouch purchase and maintenance of livestock
5. Vouch purchase and maintenance of implants, pump sets, machinery, tools, etc.
6. Verify the accounts relating to the purchases and use of seeds fertilizers, pesticides fodder, etc.
7. Vouch cultivation accounts of crops
8. Vouch muster roll register
9. Check crop yield register
10. Check register of work done
11. Vouch sale of produce and other farm products
12. Check the register of land dividend and bonus

Labour Contract Societies

The following are the items coming under the audit programme of labour contract societies:

1. Vouch share capital loan reserve fund grain implement loan and working capital revived from the government.
2. Vouch the accounts relating to each work contracted.
3. Vouch share capital loans and loans for implements disbursed to members and their recoveries in instalments out of wages payable.
4. Vouch purchase, issue and stock of construction materials.
5. Vouch payment of wages to members workers and casual workers.
6. Vouch thrift deposit accounts of members.
7. Vouch payment of bonus on wages to member workers.

Cooperative Sugar Factories

The following are the items coming under the audit programme of sugar cooperatives.

1. Vouch loans granted by industrial finance corporation.

2. Vouch the account relating to the construction of factory and office buildings and staff quarters.
3. Vouch the accounts reliant to the purchase and erection of sugar plant, and the purchase of lorries.
4. Vouch disbursements of manure loans, seed loans and nursery advances to members and their recoveries.
5. Verify the accounts relating to the purchase of seeds and manures and their distribution to the members.
6. Vouch purchase of cane from members.
7. Verify share deposits and seed deposits relieved from members.
8. Check lorry heir accounts and lorry maintenance accounts.
9. Vouch lorry hires charged to members and their recoveries.
10. Vouch purchase issue and stock of stores.
11. Vouch payment of wage to labourers employed in the mill.
12. Vouch production sale and stock of sugar and by products.

Cooperative Spinning Mills

The following are the items coming under the audit programme of cooperative spinning mills.

1. Vouch loans granted by industrial finance corporation.
2. Vouch the accounts relating to he construction of buildings the purchases and erecting of plant and machinery.
3. Vouch purchase issue and stock of cotton.
4. Vouch purchase, issue and stock of stores.
5. Check payment of wages to labourer.

6. Check the following special registers; cotton lot book mixing book cotton stock register, below room lab register, production registers, wrapping registers, yarn production doff weighment register, unreeled yarn stock register spinning production commission register, reeled yarn stock register bundle production register bundle yarn stock register bale stock register and waste cotton register.

Self-learning Activity

Try to answer the following questions on your own:

1. Discuss cooperative audit programme for Credit cooperatives.
2. What are the items for audit programme of Labour cooperatives?
3. What are items coming under the audit programme for marketing cooperatives?

Summary

- Audit programme is diary of audit process to be undertaken by the auditor. The auditor is expected to incorporate special aspects in the audit programme with regard to different types of cooperatives considering the nature of business undertaken.

18 Stages of Practical Audit Work

The practical work of the audit of a cooperative society involves four in stages:

1. Mechanical audit;
2. Administrative audit;
3. Preparation of the financial statements; and
4. Compilation of audit memorandum and schedules of defects.

The Mechanical or Financial Audit

This consists of vouching and routing checking first the entries in the cash book or day book receipts and payments are vouched carefully. The accuracy of daily balances of this book is also checked. Then the postings from the cash book in to the special ledgers and general ledger are verified. The castings of the accounts in the ledger and their balances are checked.

The object of the financial audit is to find out whether all items of receipts have been properly brought in to account and all payments are genuine and in order and to ensure that the accounts are accurate and correctly balanced. Such accuracy can be ensured only through proper examination of the books hence the financial audit should be conducted with intelligence thoroughness and utmost care.

The Administrative or Method Audit

A financial audit though the most important is not the only means by which a cooperative can be helped to keep its affairs in order. An examination of the administration of the society is also very essential this is a special feature of cooperative audit. This involves an examination in to the administrative matters and extends to all books of accounts and registers maintained by the society. The transactions and the actions of the management are examined to see whether thy are intra varies the provisions of the cooperative societies act, the rules framed under it the by laws of the society and the instruction received from the department of cooperative from time to time. The object of this examination is to find out irregularities and infringements of the act, etc and to find out how far the activities of the society conform to cooperative principles need the extent of the benefits derived by the member from the society.

The irregularities and infringements of the act the rules etc., may or may not have financial implications. For example investment of funds in a manner not prescribed in the act or rules or not approved by the registrar, grant of loans in excess of the maximum limit laid down in the by laws and purchase of the maximum limit laid down in the by laws and purchase of land or building out of general funds without the previous permission of the registrar are infringements involving financial implications. Failure to convene general meeting within the period prescribed in the by laws, failure to elect the members of the committee before he expiry of the term of office of the members of the committee and failure to give proper notice before convening a general meeting are instances of infringements having no financial implications.

In the case of infringements of the first category, the auditor has to place of concerned transactions under objection, provided the amounts involved are sustainable, if the amounts involved are trivial he should not place them under objection, but point them out in the schedules of defects, infringements having no financial implication are also pointed out in the schedules.

If, in his opinion any case is of serious nature, he must submit immediately a special report in duplicate about it to the district audit officer to be forwarded to the administrative authorities for urge remedial action.

If the accounts of the society manifest any unusual or extra ordinary features of its working they should be thoroughly investigated for instance, if with the same number of looms the production and sale in a weaver society is found to be double or triple that of the previous years, the matter will require investigation. Similarly, if the cost of cultivation per acre in a joint farming society is disproportionately high when compared with the cost in government farm or the adjoining farm of similar standard, the causes for such high cost should be enquired into. The auditor in a separate confidential report to be submitted to the district audit officer may deal with these matters.

Preparation of the Financial Statement

After completing the mechanical and administrative audits the auditor had to prepare the financial statements. These statements consist of:

1. statement of receipts and disbursements for the year;
2. the balance sheet as on the last date of the period; and
3. the profit and loss account in the case of trading societies, the profit and loss account includes the trading account also the statement of receipts and disbursement the previous years balance sheet and the list of outstanding, the balance sheet and the profit and loss account are prepared in the prescribed forms.

Audit Memorandum

Finally audit memorandum is prepared in the prescribed form, different kinds of forms have been prescribed for different types of society. The memorandum for a society should be prepared in the respective form. The various questions in the form are answered with reference to the particulars gathered from the by laws, the minute book the register and the books of account. The forms for the statement of receipts and disbursements, balance sheet and profit and loss account in the memorandum and the various annexure in the form are filed in.

Schedules of Audit Defects

The auditor should also furnish schedules of defect noted by him in the course of his audit. These are submitted to the District audit officer along with audit memorandum immediately on completion of audit. In state where this system is not in vogue the auditor sets forth in detail the defect in the concluding part of the audit memorandum under the heading general remarks. The issue of separate schedules of defects is preferable for it will enable the administrative authorities to take action to rectify them without waiting till the receipt of the audit memorandum to know the defects or before they become state by efflux of item.

In order to eliminate avoidable waste of time in rectification of defects and to avoid the schedules of defects becoming needlessly voluminous, the auditor should open a register of defects as soon as he taken up audit. The pages of its register should be divided in to two parts in the left hand side the auditor should note down in serial order all the defects noticed by him as and when he comes across them. In the evenings or whenever he breaks his work he must ask the staff or officer of the society to rectify the defects and to note down the details of rectification in the right hand side against the concerned items. He should get back the register when he resumes work and examine whether the defects have been duly rectified. In this way, most of the routine defects can be got rectified in the course of audit work only such of the defects as remain un-rectified till the cohesion of audit should be included in the schedules of defects.

In the schedules, the defects pointed out in the previous audit and still remaining unrectified should also be referred to the defects are classified and listed separately under the following heads and attached as 'schedules' to the audit memorandum.

1. All transactions which appear to be contrary to the provisions of all the act, the rules or the bylaws of the society.
2. All sums which ought to have been brought in to account but have not been done so by the society.
3. Any material impropriety or irregularity in the expenditure of in the realization of money due to the society.
4. Any money or property belonging to the society which appears to the auditor to be bad or doubtful.
5. Any other matters specified by the registrar in this behalf (see the topic on statutory provisions relating to audit).

The auditor should note in the schedules all defects with specific details. Vogue generalizations are of no use suppose it is stated signatures in vouchers must be dated "this is vogue and provides no clue for locating the defects for rectification. Therefore it should be stated as:" signatures of the payees in the following vouchers are undated: vouchers no 10: no 20 no 25............ "Similarly instead of saying adequate securities have not been obtained from the employees." the auditor should point out the exact extent of inadequacy. With reference to the standards of securities prescribed by the registrar.

The auditor should also avoid general observation such as overdue should be collected quickly " or the society should be run on better lines." in short defects stated in the schedules should be specific, clear and detailed.

Audit Report, Memorandum, and Certificate

Audit Report

Preparation of audit report is a difficult task as compared to audit work. Though the auditor has completed his work honestly and with dedication but it will be in vein if the audit report is not return in correct manner. So, audit report should be written with great care and he should be careful enough in the followings:

1. The language of audit report should be explicit and defective.
2. In audit report answers to the given questions should be correct, complete and exhaustive.
3. Objections raised in previous audit should be scrutinized and it should be seen how for they are removed.
4. Complete details should be given for the proceedings which are to be done according to cooperative principles, the Cooperative Proclamation, by-laws and the departmental directions.
5. Details of errors found in books and registers of the society should be spelt out.
6. The mistakes and errors observed during audit work should be written at proper place in the audit report.
7. The cash balance and the stock should be examined and their positions should be given in an explicit manner.
8. All vouchers of the year, other information report and the auditor should initiate audited errors and then it should be attached with the audit report.
9. If the society had received any aid then its utilization should be examined and verification should be made in the audit report.
10. Audit report should not only be critical but should also be suggestive hence suggestions should be given for the improvement in the performance of the society.

Audit Memorandum

The Cooperative Auditor is required to state the following points in the audit memorandum:

1. Audit report must be specific and accurate, based on books of account and documents examined;
2. Major and minor lapses need to be mentioned in the report;
3. The auditor must record his observations, remarks, opinions, inferences, etc.;
4. The audit report should invariable accompanied by the following list in addition to balance sheet:

   Receipts and Payments statement, trading account, profit and loss account, list of members, list of defaulters, list of stocks and dead stocks, list of creditors/debtors related statements deemed to be necessary.

5. Particulars of all transactions which appear to be contrary to me provisions of the Act, Proclamation, Rules and by-laws of the society.
6. All sums which ought to have been but have not been brought into accounts by the society.
7. Any money or property belonging to the society which appear to be bad or doubtful debts/doubtful of recovery.
8. Any other matter specified by the Registrar in this behalf.
9. The auditor is required to provide information regarding share capital, borrowings, meetings, staff structure, etc., of the society.

Audit Certificate

After writing or preparing the audit report, the auditor will prepare an audit certificate in the prescribed proforma and after duly signed, he has to submit the same to the appropriate authority for approval.

Self-Learning Activity

Try to answer the following questions on your own:

1. Discuss the stages of audit work.
2. What is schedule of defects?.
3. What are the points that must be kept in mind while preparing audit report?

Summary

- There are stages of audit work in cooperatives: mechanical or financial audit, administrative or method audit, preparation of financial statements, audit memorandum and schedule of defects.
- After completion of the audit work the auditor is required to prepare the audit report and certificate as per the cooperative proclamation and that should be approved by an appropriate authority.

19 Audit of Different Types of Cooperatives

Audit of Credit Cooperatives

Co-operative credit societies aim at promoting the economic interests of their members by encouraging them to save and by providing loans to them. They are owned and managed by their members. They grant loans to them only.

There are two kinds of co-operative credit societies, viz, agricultural credit societies and non-agricultural credit societies. Agricultural credit societies are of two types—small size societies and large-size societies.

Credit societies are required to maintain the following books and registers:

1. Minute Book;
2. Register of application for membership;
3. Admission Book;
4. Nomination Register;
5. Cash Book;
6. Receipt Book;
7. Loan Ledger;
8. Ledger of borrowings;
9. Liability Register;

10. Monthly Register of Receipt and Disbursements;
11. Register of immovable property of defaulters bought in auction by the society;
12. Register of closed Loans;
13. Register of applications for Arbitration and Execution;
14. Voucher file;
15. Register of Dividends;
16. Property Statement of members;
17. Register of Fluid Resources;
18. General Ledger.

The auditor should verify and check all the above registers and books. An example is given hereunder regarding the audit of minute book maintained by the credit cooperatives.

1. ***The audit of Minute Book:*** Minute Book is an important records. Minute Book should be referred to by the auditor in connection with the checking of entries relating to:

   (i) Collection of share capital for new shares allotted;

   (ii) refund of share capital;

   (iii) acceptance of deposits and refund thereof;

   (iv) loans borrowed from the central Bank;

   (v) disbursement of loans to members;

   (vi) investment of funds in outside securities;

   (vii) disbursement of divided on share capital;

   (viii) payment of contingent charges.

The particulars relating to the number of meetings held in a year, the names of the members of the committee of management and the name of the person or persons authorised to sign the receipts and to receive and pay cash on behalf of the society are also to be ascertained from the Minutes Book.

In the following discussions you can understand how the auditors do their duty regarding some items in credit cooperatives. Carefully go through the following discussions so that you can understand the audit process related to certain important items in credit cooperatives.

Verification of Cash Balance

This is the first item of work to be done by the auditor in conducting the mechanical audit of a society. In a village credit society the auditor should see whether the Cash Book has been written up-to-date.

He should see whether the cash balance is in the custody of the person who is authorised for this purpose in the by-laws of the society.

Vouching of Receipts

Vouching of receipts items is more difficult than vouching of payments, since direct genuine evidences are not available in all cases of receipts of money. The main evidence of receipt items consists of duplicate or counterfoil receipts.

In vouching the receipt items, the auditor should, first, note that the committee has authorised an office-bearer to sign the receipts on behalf of the society, as required in the by-laws. Then he should compare the entries in the Receipt side of the Cash Book with the corresponding counterfoils of the Receipt Book.

The auditor should see:

1. That the date, months and years of the entries in the cash Book correspond with those of the counterfoils;
2. That the name of the party, from whom the money is received and the account to which it is relating are properly recorded in the Cash Book;
3. That the amount written in figures tallies with that in words and correctly brought into the Cash Book;

4. That the receipt is properly signed by the authorised person (in the case of receipts from non-members, the receipts must be signed by such number of persons-ordinarily three-as are prescribed in the By-laws, one among them being the president or the Secretary);
5. That the receipts are in the prescribed printed forms with serial numbers;
6. That the signature of the remitter is obtained in ever receipt.

Share capital and entrance fees: The value of a share is fixed in the By-laws. Every member shall take at least one share, but no member shall take more than prescribed number of shares.

In vouching share capital and entrance fee, the auditor should consider the following points:

1. He should compare the duplicate receipts issued for the amounts of share capital and entrance fee collected from members, with the corresponding entries in the Cash Book.
2. He should see that no book adjustments without collecting share capital in cash were made. Book adjustments might be made like this: showing the amount as collected on the receipt side of the Day Book and showing on the same day on the payment side an equal amount as advances paid to members.
3. He should see that the receipts are properly prepared with necessary details and signed by the authorised person and the remitter.
4. He should examine the applications for admission if available, and the resolution of the committee in Minute Book for admission of members and allotment of share.
5. He should satisfy that the collection of share capital and entrance fees was in accordance with the by-laws. (Any

excess amount of entrance fee collected over the limit prescribed in the by-laws should be treated as a liability and refunded to the partly concerned).

6. He should note that the signatures of the members are obtained in the respective folios of the Admission book during the time of admission as well as during the time of subsequent allotment of additional shares.
7. He should see that necessary entries are made in the liability Register and General Ledgers.

Deposits

In vouching an item of deposit received, the auditor should verify the counterfoil receipt and see that the terms and other particulars of the deposit have been specified in it. In the case of fixed deposits, an application in the prescribed is obtained from the depositor and a suspense receipt is issued immediately on receipt of the amount. Later, a receipt in the form prescribed like share certificate showing among other details, the amount, rate of interest and due date and signed by those prescribed in the by-laws is issued.

Loan from Bank

While vouching this item, the auditor should attend to the following matters:

(*a*) He should verify the duplicate receipt of the society with reference to the intimation received from the bank. It should be seen that receipt issued for the loan amount has been signed by such number of members as prescribed in the By-laws.

(*b*) He must ascertain whether the committee has passed a resolution specifying the amount of loan required to be distributed to the intending borrowing members.

(*c*) He must see that the borrowing from the central bank is in accordance with the By-laws and that the loan is recommended by the Union also, if the society is based on unlimited liability.

(*d*) He must note that the total amount disbursed to members as loan is the same as that borrowed from the central bank. Any undisbursed amount should be remitted into the central bank at once towards the credit of that loan account.

(*e*) He must also see that the loan amount received from the central bank is immediately disbursed to the members without any unreasonable delay.

Loan from Government

Loans are granted by the Government to the agricultural credit societies and banks for construction of go down and office building. These loans and borrowings of other kinds made by the society should be within the maximum borrowing limit fixed in the by-laws.

He should verify the duplicate receipt of the society. He should see that the receipt has been signed by such number of members as prescribed in the By-laws. He should see whether the amount drawn out of loans, sanctioned has been immediately deposited in the Bank or utilized for the work without undue delay. He should see the various details of loans borrowed have been properly recorded in the Ledger of Borrowings.

Repayment of Loans by Members

Whenever a member remits cash on his loan account, it shall be apportioned, according to by-laws in the following order:

- *Firstly,* to execution fees, fines, postal, registration and other miscellaneous charges due from him;
- *Secondly,* interest; and
- *Thirdly,* to principal amount of the loan.

The auditor should see that the appropriation is proper according to the by-laws. He should verify the counterfoil receipts. With a view to discover misappropriation of cash received from members, it should be verified whether the signature of the borrowers or of their agents paying money on their behalf have been obtained on the counterfoils or receipts issued to them.

While vouching disbursement of loans to members the auditor should verify the following:

1. He should verify the acknowledgements of the members who received the loans. The signatures of the marks should be compared with the originals in Admission Book. Loan applications, if any, should also be verified.
2. He should see that each loan is supported by a proper constitutional sanction by the body authorised for the purpose in the by-laws.
3. He should examine the security offered for the loan and ascertain that it is adequate and proper with reference to the provisions of by-laws.
4. In the case of loans on material securities like immovable property, produce or jewels, the auditor should examine their values and satisfy himself as to their adequacy.
5. Loans on deposits should be vouched with reference to the deposit receipts surrendered by the depositors.
6. Pledge loans should be verified with reference to the agreement pledging the produce to the society. The auditor should see that the produce has been placed in the custody of the society. He should also see that the loan amounts issued do not exceed the prescribed percentage of the values of produces pledged.
7. He should examine the bonds executed by the borrowers and see whether they are proper and regular. In the case of surety loans, the signatures of both the borrower and the surety should have been obtained in the bonds. In the case of mortgage of immovable property, the bond should have been duly registered and an encumbrance certificate obtained.

8. He should note that the purposes and the periods for which the loans are granted are proper according to the provisions.
9. In the case of loans exceeding $.250 granted by an unlimited liability society, the sanction by the concerned central bank should be examined.
10. The auditor should see whether the loan amounts have been actually disbursed or partly disbursed and partly adjusted to previous dues. He should report the latter cases.

Shares in Other Bank or in Other Societies

He should verify the receipts issued by the other bank or the society concerned for the payment of installments of share capital. He should also see that the Investment has been made with the approval of the general body of the members. In the case of fully paid-up shares, the share certificates issued by the society concerned should also be examined.

Repayment of Loans to Banks

Remittance into the banks towards loan account may be made either:

(i) in person or

(ii) by money order or

(iii) by a bank draft

The auditor should examine the final receipts issued by the banks as well as the tentative receipts and see that the details of the appropriation made by the bank are correctly entered in the cash book of the society. If such details are not noted in the cash book, the auditor should himself do the same so as to avoid further reference to the final receipts in connection with the preparation on the statement of Receipts and Disbursements wherein, the amount of principal and that of the interest paid of the banks should be separately given. The auditor should compare the date of receipt of money by the central bank with the date on which the amount was taken for remittance. Any discrepancy should be examined and reported.

Repayment of loans to Government — The auditor should verify the chalans and see whether they bear the seal of the Treasury and the number and the signature of the treasury officer.

Establishment and Contingent Charges

(a) *Establishment*

The auditor should vouch the establishment charges with reference to the Acquittance Roll. He should verify the particulars and check the castings. He should see that the amount paid to each is in accordance with the amount of scale of pay and allowance fixed by the committee subject to the budget allotment. Any modification in the scale or allowances or increments should be properly sanctioned by the committee. Any commitments exceeding the budget allotment should be approved by the general body of members. He should see that the appointments are in accordance with the By-laws or special subsidiary Regulations framed by the committee and circulars issued by the registrar from time to time.

(*b*) *Contingent Charges*

In vouching contingent charges, the auditor should not only verify the voucher for payments but also satisfy himself that they are regular and necessary and backed by the constitutional sanction as required in the By-laws.

Audit of Industrial/Weavers Cooperatives

Industrial co-operative are voluntary associations of artisans or craftsmen organised for the promotion of their economic interests.

Production and sales co-operatives include weaver's co-operative societies, coir societies, pot makers' co-operatives, basket makers' co-operatives, mat-weavers' co-operatives and other village and handicraft co-operatives.

Special Registers and Books

Besides the registers and books that are common to all societies, a weavers society maintains the following additional special registers and books:

1. Raw Material Issue Register;
2. Raw Material Stock Register;
3. Finished Goods Receipt Register;
4. Sales Classification Sheet;
5. Sales Register;
6. Wages Register;
7. Raw Material Recovery Register;
8. Finished Goods Stock Register;
9. Personal Ledger;
10. Cash Advance Register;
11. Thrift Deposits Register;
12. Consignment Ledger;
13. Consignment Invoice Books; and
14. Job Card.

The following are the items to be verified by the auditor:

Raw Material Issue Register — The auditor should verify each item of entries made in this register. He should verify whether signatures of members were obtained in the register, whether materials were issued to members only and whether the members who were issued materials were genuine workers.

Raw Material Stock Register — The auditor should verify this register thoroughly with reference to inward cash bills and invoice and Raw Material Issue Register and verify the balances.

Finished Goods Receipt Register — The auditor should verify the entries made in this register with reference to the duplicates of Job Cards or Appraiser's Tickets, and see that finished goods received from members had been properly brought into account.

Sales Register — The auditor should verify this register with reference to duplicates of invoices and cash bills.

Sales Classification Sheets — The auditor should verify the sales classification sheets with reference to duplicates of invoices and cash bills. He should check the totals of the sheets, and see that they have been correctly posted into Finished Goods Stock Register.

Wages Register — The auditor should verify this register with reference to duplicates of job cards or appraiser's tickets.

Sets Outstanding Register or Material Recovery Register — The auditor should check this register with reference to Raw material Issue Register and Job Card. He should see whether any sets are outstanding for a long time.

Finished Goods Stock Register — The auditor should verify this register with reference to Finished Goods Receipt Register and sales classification sheets.

Personal Ledger - The auditor should verify the personal account of each member with reference to above registers. He should check the postings and balances.

Cash Advance Register — The auditor should verify this register with reference to Day Book and Job cards are Appraiser's Tickets, and see that signatures of members have been obtained in their respective folios. He should see that advances are promptly recovered from members.

Thrift Deposits Register — the auditor should verify the entries with reference to duplicates of appraiser's tickets.

Consignment — The auditor should verify and countersign it and attach it to the audit memorandum.

Job Cards or Appraiser's Tickets — The auditor should verify these cards or tickets and check the calculations of wages with reference too approved schedule of wages maintained by the society. He should see that signatures of members have been obtained in the cards or tickets.

Vouching of Special Items

Share Capital Loan

The auditor should go through the order of sanction and the intimation of withdrawal of amount and see whether the amount has been properly brought into account and adjusted to members' share capital accounts.

Purchases of Raw Materials

The auditor should study the system of internal checking in vogue in respect of.

Rebate on Sales

The auditor should verify the re-imbursement with reference to the order of sanction and the intimation of withdrawal and see that the amount is properly brought into the account.

Audit of Other Types of Cooperatives

Audit of Consumer Cooperatives

The following are the items to be verified by the auditor in consumer cooperatives:

1. **Purchases** — As regards the placing and execution of orders for purchase of different commodities and maintenance of accounts thereof, there should prevail an efficient system of internal check in the society.

   The auditors should satisfy himself that the system of internal check as regards purchases is thorough and efficient and that there is no scope for committing any mistakes or frauds in this respect. He should verify the invoices with reference to the order book and the Goods Inward Register and check the postings to the purchase, Issue and Stock Register. In respect of credit purchases which are only occasional in a co-operative stores society, the auditor should scrutinize the bills very carefully.

2. **Expenses or purchases or incidental Charges** — Vouchers relating to the different kinds of incidental charges such as Railway freight, cartage, lorry fare, travelling expenses, etc, incurred on purchases have to be carefully, verified.

3. **Price fixation** — the retail sales prices of articles are fixed by a sub-committee appointed by the Board. Generally, the purchase committee itself acts' as the price-fixing committee.

   The auditor should verify the calculations in the price list and also satisfy himself that salesmen have sold the goods as per the prices noted in the price.

4. **Sales** — Sales are made by the salesman according to the selling prices fixed by the purchases or price-fixation committee.

   A percentage check of sales chits may be considered adequate only in cases where the compartmental system of stocking goods is closely adhered to, and where deficits in stocks with the salesmen are correctly ascertained and recoveries for shortage are promptly made.

5. **Sales-Tax** — Sales paid is an expenditure incurred after the sales are made. Therefore it is an indirect expenditure like carriage outward. Sales tax collected from members may be included in the sales or accounted separately.

6. **Trade deposits** — Trade deposits are peculiar to a co-operative stores society. They are deposits of money made by members with the society against which credits sales might be made to them.

The auditor should verify trade deposits with reference to the duplicate receipts and the resolution of the Board accepting them. The adjustments of deposits for the value of purchases made by the depositors accounts. The pass-books of some of the depositors should be called for and verified with the books of the society.

7. **Empties** — A stores society makes its purchases in bulk from wholesalers or manufactures. Goods are received in various kinds of containers such as gunny bags, tins and wooden boxes. These containers are emptied when goods contained for. A register of empties should be maintained.

   He should verify the stock of empties on hand and compare the actual stock with the book stock as per the register of empties. He should report on the discrepancy, if any, in his Audit Memorandum or Schedules of Defects.

8. **Members' credit purchase Register** — This register is maintained by employees' stores societies whose by-laws permit credit sales to members on the guarantee of their employer. The auditor should verify the register and see whether recoveries are made promptly. He should call for the pass books of at least a few members and compare the entries therein with the corresponding entries in the register. The object of this comparison is to ensure that credit sales accounts are perfect.

9. **Conversion Register** — This is maintained by a store having processing activities such as hulling of rice, production of oil, manufacture of coffee powder, etc. The auditor should see that liability percentage of quantity-finished product to that of raw sales tax is not less than normal standard yield. He should also compare the cost price of finished product with its market price and see if the processing has been profitable.

   The postings into from this register should be checked with reference to raw material stock ledger, cash book and finished product stock ledger. He should check the calculation of cost price of finished product. He should check the sale of by product.

10. **Register of Bonus on Purchases** — A certain rate percent of the profits of a stores society is distributed among the members by way of bonus (or dividend) on purchases made by them. The auditor should verify the entries in the register with sales chits. He should also verify the calculation of bonus of purchases. He should see that the rate the bonus is in accordance with the by-laws of the society and that the bonus has been declared by the general body of the members with reference to their signature obtained in the register or the separate vouchers obtained from them.

11. **Verification of stock, Depreciation and Deficit in Stock** — The periodical verification of stock is a very important work in a co-operative stores society. According to the by-laws, the stock of a society should be verified at the end of each quarter by two or more directors appointed by a resolution of the Board.

    The auditor should see whether stocks have been verified at the end of each quarter. He should study the reasonableness of depreciation allowed by the Board with reference to total conditions and depreciation allowed by local merchants. He should see whether deficits in excess or normal depreciation allowed had been recovered from the employees concerned.

12. **Condemned Articles** — At times, goods may get deterioration due to stocking or damaged while handling.

    The auditor should verify the accounts relating to sale of condemned goods with reference to the resolution of the Board for the purpose. He should also study the circumstances of thee case.

13. **Stock Taking and Valuation of Stock** — Stock-taking is done in the immediate presence of a department officer

once in a half-years, that is, for the half-years ending 30th June and 31st December.

The auditor who conducts the final audit of the stores can use for his audit purposes the final figure as found in the stock statement copy with the District Audit Officer.

Administrative Audit

The following are related to administrative audit in consumer cooperatives:

Purchases — When purchases are made on credit, the auditor should scrutinize the invoice very carefully and make sure that credit bills are not converted into cash bills and the amounts misappropriated. To be sure, the auditor should get statements of accounts direct from the suppliers.

Sales — Regarding credit sales, the following points should be examined by the auditor:

1. There should be provision in the by-laws for sale on credit.
2. In employee's societies, the society should get undertakings from the pay disbursing officers agreeing to recover the dues from the salary of members to whom credit sales are made.
3. The amount outstanding against a member for credit sales made too him should not any time exceed the credit limit fixed by the Board.
4. The society should get an indent or an acknowledgement duly signed by a member for the issue of articles to him on credit basis; or his signature should be obtained in the invoice. Unless this is done, it might not be legally possible to recover the arrears.
5. It would facilitate matters if the members are supplied with pass books where entries are made as when supplies are made on credit and recoveries are also recorded in them.

The auditor should see whether any article remaining unsold for over six months. If so, he should enquire into the reason and see whether prompt action was taken to dispose off it before it got deteriorated.

Salesmen's liability — The auditor should check the salesmen's liability register and see whether the signature of the salesmen was obtained every time goods were issued to him or he remitted the sale proceeds.

Final Account and Balance Sheet

Final Account —The final account of a co-operative stores society consist of two sections:

1. Trading Account; and
2. Profit and Loss Account

The auditor should verify the correctness of each item included in the final account and see that it is prepared accurately.

Balance Sheet — The auditor should verify the various items of assets and liabilities as explained previously. The auditor should also check the statements of account received from the suppliers and satisfy himself that balance shown in the ledger agree with the figures of the statement.

Audit of Housing Cooperatives

There are four main types of housing societies:

1. ordinary building societies;
2. house building societies;
3. house construction societies; and
4. house tenancy societies.

Special items to be audited in Housing Cooperatives

The following are special items to be verified by an auditor.

Purchase of site

The auditor has to see whether such agreements have been obtained from members.

Issue of loan

He has to verify only the acknowledgement given by the Registrar for having received the bonds on behalf of government.

House-construction

The auditor should see whether hire-purchase agreement has been executed by each member for the allotment of the house. He should verify the calculation of interest and installment amount and see whether members pay their installments regularly. He should see that suitable actions as prescribed in the by-laws and in the agreements have been taken against members who fail to pay installments or to keep up the terms of agreements.

Audit of Marketing Cooperatives

The auditor should verify following additional ledgers:

1. Stock Register of produce received on agency basis.
2. Stock Register of produce pledged.
3. Auction Register
4. Tender Sheet.
5. Stock Register of produce purchased and sold.
6. Auction or sales slip.
7. Marketing Panchayatdar's or agents' personal ledger.
8. Stock receipts issued by marketing panchayatdars.
9. Stock registers of fertilizers and other agricultural requirements.

The auditor should see that sale of members' produce has been made to their best advantage. In the case of auction sales, he should verify whether the procedure laid down in the by-laws, or regulations or in the resolutions of the Board of Directors has been observed and the auction was conducted with the consent of members. He should verify with reference to the auction slip whether all the dues to the society under various have have been recovered.

He should check the accounts relation to distribution of fertilizers, etc. as agents to the District Supply and Marketing Society. He should see whether periodical accounts are rendered to the district society and sale-proceeds are promptly remitted.

The auditor should physically verify stocks of produce and fertilizers etc, and see if their condition is good. In the case of stock pledged for loans advanced, the auditor should see that its value is adequate for coverage and that in case of appreciable fall in value, additional security has been obtained from the borrower. Needless to say, the auditor should also examine if the society has secured effective custody of the produce pledged by the members.

Audit of Milk Supply Cooperatives

The auditor should vouch loans issued to members and see if the instalments are recovered regularly out of sale-proceeds of milk and if the society verified the animals periodically till the loans are cleared. If any loan is overdue, the reasons should be investigated. He should verify the Milk Record Register and see that all the milk supplied by members has been duly brought into account. He should call for a few members' pass book and compare their entries with corresponding entries in the Milk Record Register. He should see that total quantity supplied to union tallies with the quantity acknowledged by it. He should vouch supply of fodder and other articles to members and the recovery of cost out of sale proceeds and the payment of net sale proceeds to members. A few members' pass books should be called for and checked by him.

The auditor should, then, verify the Recoveries and payments Register in which the quantity of milk supplied by each member, the amount to be paid, recoveries made towards commission, loans, fines, etc., and net amount paid to him are recorded. He should verify this register with reference to the Milk Record Register and Day Book. He should see that each member has put his signature for the net amount paid to him.

The auditor should verify the invoices for the milk supplied to the union. The invoice is prepared in triplicate and presented in duplicate to the union with milk. The union returns one copy to the society acknowledging receipt of the quantity actually received by it. The auditor should verify the copies of invoices retained in the society with the copies with acknowledgment received from the union.

Audit of Labour Contract Cooperatives

Labour contract societies are societies of work from the public works department and private parties and execute them through members and hired labour, if necessary. They pay wages to members and bonus on wages out of profits. They aim at Elimination middlemen's (i.e., contractor's) profits. They get different forms of aid from the government, such as interest free share capital loan of a certain amount to each member, interest free loan for members for purchase of minor implements, working capital loan, reserve fund loan etc.

State aid: The auditor should verify the orders of sanctioned aids and see whether the funds are properly utilized. Regarding share capital and implement loans sanctioned to members, the society should execute an indemnity for the amount, offering all its assets as security for the loan. He should see whether loan amounts were properly utilized and loan instalments were promptly repaid.

Contract of work: the society should maintain a contract Register in which each work that is taken up is allotted a separate page for recording its details such as nature of work, amount of contract, mode of execution (i.e., by direct labour or sub- contract), amount spend and progress of work. The auditor should check this register and see whether works are executed properly and according to the terms of contract.

Employment of labour: The society should study the working of internal check as regards employment of labour and calculation and payment of wages. He should see that wages have been paid only to the persons actually engaged in work. He should see whether Muster-Roll and the wage sheets have been properly certified by responsible officials. He should check the calculations in the wage sheets and vouch weekly payments with the corresponding entries in the cash Book. He should see whether thrift deposits at the rate prescribed in the by-laws have been deducted from the wages and credited to the concerned members' thrift deposit accounts.

He should study the extent to which members were benefited. He should see that non-members were employed only when it was necessary to do so.

He should see that the work-in-progress as on the last date of the year and the other assets were valued properly.

Audit of Sugar Cooperatives

Co-operative sugar factories are processing societies organized by sugarcane producers with a view to derive the benefits of processing.

Apart from regular items, the following special items are to be verified by the auditor in a sugar cooperative factory.

Cane Purchase Register

The auditor should verify cane purchases Registers with reference to cane weighment sheets and see that all purchases have been brought into account. He should check suppliers accounts in the cane suppliers Ledgers with reference to Purchases Registers and Sub-day Book. He should get the balances as on the last day of the year confirmed by the suppliers concerned.

Share Deposit Register — The auditor should verify the register with reference to sub-day Book and Admission Register.

Cane Seed Deposit Register — The auditor should verify this Register with Sub-Day Book and honoured seedling permits.

Press Mud Deposit Register — The auditor should check this register with Day Book.

Self-learning Activity

Try to answer the following questions on your own:

1. What are points to be considered by the auditor with respect to vouching disbursement of loans to members?
2. What is the duty of an auditor in vouching special items in an industrial cooperative?
3. What are special items to be verified by the auditor in a sugar cooperative?
4. How an auditor can verify the items in a consumer stores?

Summary

- The audit process and the items to be verified by an auditor in credit cooperatives, industrial/weavers cooperatives, and other cooperatives like consumer, housing, marketing, milk supply, labour contract cooperatives, and sugar cooperatives are discussed in this chapter.

20 Cooperative Audit Stages
Vouching and Routine Checking

Stages/Phases of Audit Work

Before discussing the various processes in cooperative audit, you must know the stages involved in cooperative audit work.

The audit process has four stages or phases. They are:

1. vouching of day book;
2. checking the ledger postings;
3. verification of final accounts and balance sheet; and
4. Prepartion and submission of audit report and audit certificate.

The following figure depicts a clear picture of the audit process:

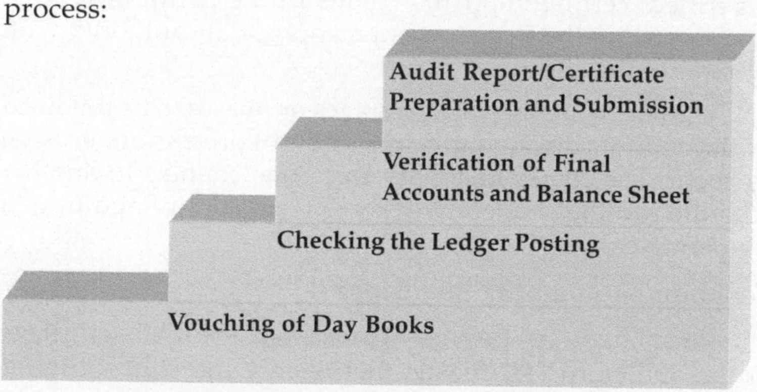

Fig. 20.1: **Stages/Phases of Audit Work**

***Stage 1:* Vouching of Day Books**

The first stage in the audit work is extensive vouching of day books of the cooperative society. The entries made in the books of original entry are verified with all available document evidences in order to see if they are in an order, genuine and constitutional to ensure that the books of accounts are correct and reflect nothing but truth.

***Stage 2:* Checking the Ledger Postings**

The second stage in the audit work is the checking of ledger postings. After vouching of day books is over the ledger postings are verified and the arithmetical accuracy of accounts is attested by the agreement of the statement of receipts ad payments for the period under review.

***Stage 3:* Verification of Final Accounts and Balance Sheet**

At this stage, the verification of final accounts ie., trading and profit & loss accounts, and balance sheet is done to arrive at the true financial position of the cooperative business as on the date effected. After the examination is finalized the auditor verify the existence of assets and check their valuations.

***Stage 4:* Audit Report/Certificate Preparation and Submission**

Finally, the correctness of balance sheet and final accounts is verified, certified and the results of the auditing process are reported to the Registrar or an appropriate authority with all required enclosures.

The above are the various stages or phases to be followed by the auditors during the course of audit process undertaken by them. The stages may vary from one country to another according to the cooperative law and practice of auditing in cooperatives.

Vouching — Meaning and Steps

Vouching is the essence of audit and the first step/stage in the audit process, means that testing the truth of items appearing in the books of original entry.

Vouching may be defined as "an examination of every transaction of a cooperative business with relevant documents and other evidences with a view to finding out if it genuine and bonafide".

Vouching connotes an extensive investigation it aims at ascertaining whether a transaction is in order, has been properly authorized and is correctly recorded in the books of original entry. It traces each entry to its source and explores its implications and circumstances. It studies the authentication and orderliness of records. The enquiry should not confine itself to the entries alone, because they can not constitute the final 'say' in the matter. The entries reflect only such information as the book-keeper intense to disclose, and his intension may sometimes be contrary to reality. So real truth cannot be ascertained by more examination of entries so enquiry should go further. It should go beyond the books and external evidences should be examined.

Steps in Vouching

There are eight stages or steps in vouching. The following diagram presents the stages involved in vouching process:

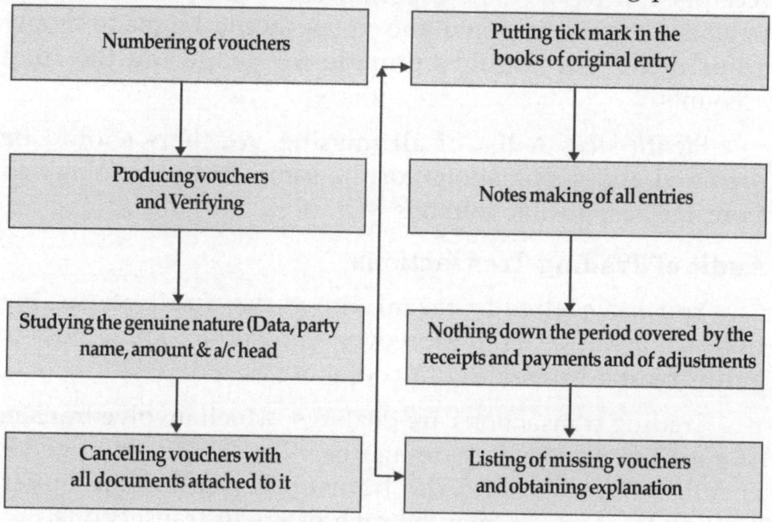

Fig. 20.2: **Steps in Vouching**

First step: The auditor should see that all vouchers are numbered consecutively and safely filed in the order in which the corresponding entries appear on the original record.

Second step: All the vouchers for the period under review should be produced at the time and the auditor should verify vouchers for definite period at the time.

Third step: The auditor should study the genuine nature of each voucher; he should examine the date of the voucher, party's name to whom it is addressed, the amount and the account head.

Fourth step: The auditor should cancel the vouchers with all documents attached to it when he putting his initial on its face duly passes it.

Fifth step: The entry in books should be ticked when the corresponding voucher is passed.

Sixth step: While examining vouchers careful notes should be made of all entries.

Seventh step: While examining vouchers for periodical receipts and payments the period covered by the receipt or payment should be noted and notes should be made of any adjustment that should be made for preparing the final accounts.

Eighth step: A list of all missing vouchers should be prepared and explanations for the same should be obtained from the responsible persons.

Audit of Trading Transactions

You have already learnt about the audit of trading transactions in general. Moreover, you should know how to audit trading transaction in cooperatives.

Trading transactions are dealings, which involve transfer of goods from one party to another. The transferor of goods is called the seller and the transferee is called the buyer. Trading transactions may be cash or credit transactions.

They refer to only such goods as are intended for resale, i.e., goods in which the business is carried on. Under double entry book keeping credit purchases and sales are recorded in separate purchase book and sales book respectively. In cooperative account keeping they are entered in the day book itself and the details are entered in the Register concerned.

Purchase

The Auditor should study the system and devote more attention on weak points if any. He should check the invoices with the corresponding entries in the purchase book, and or/ day book and cancel them after duly passing them. He should test the items of purchases with the order placed and goods inward register. The calculations in the invoices should be tested and check at random fraud might also be committed by various means and therefore auditor should take much care in examining vouchers with the entries the day book related to purchase of goods.

Purchase Returns

The auditor should check the returns outward book or day book. The auditor should see that those items are properly dealt with. He should also vouch the book and relevant correspondent entries and also check the castings and postings of the book.

Hire and Instalment Purchases

The auditor should examine the actual hire purchase agreement or agreement to pay by installments and ascertain the particulars regarding the capital value the rate of interest, the amount of instalment as the case may be. The vouchers for the payment of the installments should be inspected.

Sales

As regards sales there may be two kinds of defalcations namely, omission of sales and inclusion of false items of sales. The auditor should investigate the system adopted in executing orders for supply of goods. Invoices should be checked with the sales book on daybook as the case may be and the entries there in should be compared with the goods outward register. He should also check whether any items of sales of old assets have been passed through the sales book.

Sales Returns

The auditor should check the sales returns book or daybook with credit notes, corresponding debit notes received from parties corresponding and goods inward register.

Packages and Empties

Auditor should verify packages and empties with respective invoices. He may also compare the rates at which the packages and empties have been sold with the prevailing market rates.

Checking of Ledgers

The auditor should check the postings into the concerned head of accounts in the ledger and the daily balances, monthly totals of Receipts and payments columns and their progressive totals. While examining nominal accounts the auditor should see that postings were made under proper heads of accounts. Similarly while examining asset accounts the auditors should see that no items of revenue nature like repairs etc. is posted in to them.

The auditor should verity the postings in the various special ledgers (Admission book, Loan ledger, ledger of Borrowings, Liability Register, Register of dividend etc) and their balances and reconcile them with the corresponding balances in the General Ledger.

Checking of Receipts and Payments Statements

The auditor should verity RPS with reference to the totals of the two sides of the accounts in the General ledger and the opening and closing balances of the day book for the period.

Final Adjustments

The basic principle govern the preparation of the final account is that it should include only the actual amount pertaining to the period under various revenue accounts. This calls for some adjustments. There may be certain items of expenses such as rent, interest, salaries, wages etc. that belong to the period under review and have accrued, but have not paid and, therefore, do not appear in the accounts. The amounts accrued are added to the respective items in the final accounts and also included on the liability side of the balance sheet under the respective heads.

In contrast to these outstanding expenses, there may be expenses that are usually paid in advance, such as insurance, rates, taxes etc. This is done by deducting unexpended amount should be included as an item on the assets side of the balance sheet.

Income accrued on the due but not received at the times of balancing are brought in to account by passing necessary adjustment entries. The amounts accrued are added to the respective incomes in the final account and also shown as assets in the balance sheet.

Income received in advance, if any, should be adjusted properly. The adjustment is made by deducting the amount from the particular nominal account and also by showing it on the liability side of the balance sheet.

Outstanding Expenses and Prepaid Expenses

The following are the items to be audited by the auditor as regards outstanding expenses and prepaid expenses.

Expenses Due

The omission to bring any outstanding liability for expenses into the accounts with affect the profit and loss account. The auditor should therefore, see that all outstanding liabilities for expenses for the period under audit are dealt with properly. The following are the common instances of outstanding liabilities.

Wages

The auditor should test the calculation and see that the amount of wages due is shown on the liability side of the balance sheet.

Rent, Rates etc.

The auditor should examine the ledger accounts, demand notice and a acknowledgements carefully noting the period covered by each payment and see that any accrued and unpaid amount to the date of the balance sheet is brought in as a liability.

Salaries

The acquittance roll on salaries book should be examined noting the period covered by the payments and it should be seen if the amount outstanding for period has been provided for:

Miscellaneous Expenses

Total should be added to miscellaneous expense in the final account and then included in the liability side of the balance sheet. The auditor should examine whether such provision and entry is made or not.

Interest Payable

The auditor with reference to the loan agreements and the acknowledgement for interest actually paid should examine this.

Prepaid Expenses

At the time of balancing there may be some items of expenses, such as rent, rates, advertisement, insurance etc, which are paid in advance, covering a period beyond the date of balance sheet. The auditor should examine the adjustment entries as well as vouchers for such payments and verify the calculations.

Accrued income and Income received in advance

The following are the items to be audited by the auditor as regards accrued income and income received in advance.

Rent Receivable

All items of rent receivable from tenants due on accrued to the date of the balance sheet should be calculated and brought in to accounts. This is done by adding the accrued amount received in the final account and it is also shown as an asset in the Balance sheet.

Interest and Dividend

Interest accrued on loans should be calculated and brought into account only interest accrued and overdue should not be included in the profit and loss account. This adjustment should be verified with reference to the bonds and loans account. Similarly dividends on shares in other cooperatives may be calculated and brought into accounts. This should be checked with reference to the share certificates and dividend warrants.

Commission Receivable

Commission due and accrued to the date of the balance sheet should be brought in to account. The auditor should examine the basis of calculation in order to satisfy himself that the amount brought into account is correct.

Income Received in Advance

It is essential to apportion any income received in advance and only the portion relating to the current year should be brought into the profit and loss account and balance sheet Advertisement charges is received by News papers concern and insurance premium received by insurance company. The auditor should examine such nominal accounts, noting the periods covered by them, and see that the amount pertaining to the un-expired period has been properly calculated or not.

Differed Revenue Expenditure

Revenue expenses of large amounts, the benefits of which are lightly to accrue over a number of years beyond the year in which they were incurred are used to the temporarily capitalized and return off equitably during those years. They are called differed revenue expenses.

Example

(i) *Alternations to plant:* Sometimes heavy expenditure may be incurred for including plant and machinery. This expenditure includes the earning capacity of the business. Therefore it is not wholly charging to current revenue. It is written off over a short period of years. The auditor should study the nature of expenditure and examine the reasonable time of the period of years over which the expenditure is to be written off.

(ii) *Advertising:* The auditor should verity the expenditure by examining vouchers correspondence etc. and see that it is carried forward over a reasonable length of time only.

Depreciation

Depreciation has been as a loss or shrinkage in the use value of an asset. The cause for deprecation may be internal or external. Internal cause is natural to or inherent in the asset itself Eg., wear and tear. Depreciation arises due to this cause in the case of such assets as plant and machinery, motor lorries, furniture and fittings, buildings etc. External causes are the operation of forces outside the assets itself. An asset like a plant may become obsolete i.e, out of date due to invention of an improved type and consequently losses its use value. Depreciation is caused by effluxion of time in the case of assets like leases, which become valueless after the end of the definite period.

Object of Depreciation

The object of providing for depreciation is three fold namely:

(*a*) To arrive at the correct profit or loss;

(*b*) To make the balance sheet represent the real state of affairs; and

(*c*) To keep the capital invested in the acquisition of fixed assets intact.

Methods for providing depreciation

You have already studied all the methods of depreciation, while we were discussing about the methods of depreciation in general audit. The same methods can be applied in cooperative also. Just to recall you the methods of depreciation are listed out hereunder:

1. The fixed instalment or straight line method
2. The diminishing balance method
3. The annuity method
4. The depreciation fund system
5. The revaluation method
6. The insurance policy method
7. The depreciation cum requires and renewals method.

The Auditors Duty as regards depreciation

The auditor must remember the fact that the question of depreciation is closely conducted with the balance sheet. He has no technical knowledge of such assets as plant and machinery. He should study the circumstances of each case, ascertain the accuracy of the estimation of the working life of assets. The opinions and conclusion of experts should be accepted and taken into consideration. His main responsibility is to satisfy himself that the amount of depreciation is both adequate and accurate.

Bad and Doubtful debts

Debts arise on account of given credit transactions or direct advance of loans. Debts that could not be recovered are considered to be bad debt and debt of doubtful recovery are called doubtful debts. The accounts of debts considered to be bad on doubtful debts should be transferred to the register of bad/doubtful debts. In respect of doubtful debts reserve should be created according to their estimated value.

Auditors Position as for Bad and Doubtful Debts

After careful investigation if the auditor feels that the reserve is insufficient he should try to convince the concerned authorities and to induce them to make the additional reserve required as per his opinion. The auditor should therefore exercise due care and reasonable consideration in this regard.

Contingent Liabilities

The contingent liabilities are liabilities which have not arisen or accrued but may arise in future on the happening of certain events. They may or may not involve payment of money. The following are some instances of continent liabilities:

1. Liability on Bills receivable discounted and not matured
2. Liability for calls on partly paid up shares
3. Liability on pending litigation
4. Liability under a contract Guarantee
5. Liability for penalties under contract.

The contingent liabilities are dealt with in two different ways. The first way is to simply mention the nature of the liability on the face of the Balance sheet by way of the footnote. The second way is to create a reserve for the purpose.

Auditor's Duty

The auditor should examine various books of accounts necessary to point out the contingent liabilities (Example: Bills, registered minutes book etc). The auditor should examine into such liabilities and see that adequate reserves are created for more liabilities where a loss is anticipated and that other liabilities are disclosed in the balance sheet by way of a foot note where there is no contingent liability is better for the auditor to get a certificate to that effect from a responsible officer of the undertaking.

Routine Checking, and Methods of Checking and Locating Errors

Routine Checking

Routine checking as very name implies mechanical work. Yet, it is an important part and task of audit work, say the auditor's work. It constitutes checking of calculations of bills, vouchers, etc., castings of books of original entry, postings in ledgers, castings of ledger accounts and balancing of cashbook and ledger accounts. This process of routine checking can ascertain the arithmetical accuracy of the books of accounts.

Auditor should make routine checking interesting and lively by his imagination and intelligence. The extent of routine checking depends on the system of book keeping and internal check in force. In the case of small business concerns having no internal check, the whole of the castings and postings should be checked. In a large concern having some sort of internal check, the auditor need not check all castings and postings, but adopt 'test check'.

The amount of check should be conducted and the extent to which the internal check is realized on this respect should be judged by the auditor in the light of his experience and of the circumstances of the particular case. He should not endeavour to do as little checking as possible but rather to do as much ha can.

However, much time should not be devoted to routine check. Since it would reveal nothing but clerical errors and very simple frauds. It will seldom disclose errors of principle and clever frauds. They could be discovered only by intelligent enquiries and examination of the books themselves.

Methods of Checking and Locating Errors

The following steps may be taken one after another until the errors that cause the difference are located:

1. The Grand totals of both sides of the statement should be rechecked and the exact amount of the difference should be ascertained.
2. It should be seen that the amounts of opening and closing balances are correctly included in the Receipts and payments side respectively.
3. Figures, which are not clearly written, should be examined.
4. The totals and carrying forwards of ledges accounts should be checked.
5. The nature of the difference may provide a clue for locating the error if the amount of differences is wrong sum. It is probable that some errors might have committed in castings.
6. If all these attempts file all the postings, castings and carrying forward should be completely rechecked.

The errors so located should be rectified the mistakes in castings should be rectified by striking off the wrong figures and writing the correct figures. Omissions in postings should be rectified making the postings concerned.

Self-learning Activity

Try to answer the following questions on your own:

1. Define vouching and what are the steps involved?
2. What are trading transactions that are to be audited?
3. What is the need for final adjustments?

4. How will you audit prepaid expenses?
5. What is deferred revenue expense? Give examples.
6. What is routine checking?
7. What is the method of locating errors?

Summary

- Vouching and routine checking is done by the auditors since they are the basic essence of audit process. Different items are to be checked.
- By routine checking the auditors can locate the errors.

21 Verification and Valuation of Assets and Liabilities

Verification of Assets and Liabilities

After vouching various books of accounts auditor has to turn his attention to the most important stage of his work namely verification of assets. If vouching is necessary to ascertain the correctness of transactions, the verification of assets is necessary to find out the truth of the balance sheet.

The verification of assets means an examination as such evidences as will satisfy the auditor that all those assets, which ought to exist at the date of the balance sheet were actually in existence on that particular date.

Steps in Verification Process

1. The auditor's duty with regard to verification of assets is four fold. First, he should ascertain what assets ought to exist at the date of the balance sheet. The entries in the books of accounts (Provided they are correctly recorded) will disclose the assets which ought to be in the possession of the undertaking.
2. The auditor must verify by actual expectation or otherwise what such assets have existed actually at the date of the balance sheet.
3. He should see that all the assets appeared at their proper values.
4. He should ascertain that all assets were free from any changes other than those disclosed in the books.

Verification of Various Assets

1. Cash on hand

There is no short-cut method for the verification of cash on hand. The verification should be done by actual counting. Balance verified should be compared with the balance as per the book. Apart from verifying cash balance the auditor should ascertain that cash balance on any day is not larger than i.e. normally required. If so, he should make careful enquiries in this regard.

2. Cash at Bank

Bank balance at date of the balance sheet is verified by means of the examination of the entries in the pass book. The cash balance should be checked with the pass book and the two balances agreed by means of a Reconciliation statement. The auditor should obtain the certificate directly from the banker so as to provide the production of dummy pass book fraudulently.

3. Investments

The auditor should demand a schedule of investments. The schedule should contain particulars of each investment, its cost price and the value at which is taken to the balance sheet. The schedule should be verified with the investment register and the consigned ledger accounts. The basis of valuation depends on purpose for which the investments are held Investments of permanent nature with value at cost price temporary and fluctuations in value can be ignored. In all cases the basis of valuation should be mentioned on the phase of balance sheet.

Verification of different classes of Investments may be done as detailed below:

1. Debentures, registered stocks and shares

In the case of debentures, registered stocks and shares the name of hold is entered in the register of the issuing concern and bond or certificate as case may be is issued in the name of the holder. The auditor should examine the broker's bought note and the certificates or the bonds. He should see that they have been properly executed and sealed. He should see that proper sanction is made by the General Body of the society. The auditor should also examine the allotment letters and the receipts for the payment of instalments.

2. Bearer securities and share warrants to bearer

These must be examined by actual inspection of the bonds and the interest on dividend coupons attached herein.

3. Book debts

The book balances should be verified with statements of confirmation received from debtors which should be directly attested to the auditors. The status of each account should be carefully examined and adequate provision for bad and doubtful debts should be made.

4. Bills Receivables

The auditor should first ascertain bills on hand at the date of balance sheet from the Bills receivable account in the ledger. In examining the bills it should be seen that they are drawn properly and stamped and not overdue. If verification is done after that date bills that have been met or discounted subsequently should be verified by vouching the cash received. The auditor should examine through a certificate to that effect obtained from the bankers. In case of bills likely to be dishonored sufficient provision should be made for loss likely to arrive. In respect of bills discounted a note of contingent liability should appear on the balance sheet.

5. Stock in trade

The auditor should verify and value stock in trade by examining the document evidences related to such items and he should see that the entries made in the register of stock in trade or stock register maintained by the societies.

6. Land and Buildings (freehold and leasehold properly)

The title deeds should be examined; the last deed should be examined to see that the property has been duly conveyed to his clients or their trustees. For this purpose encumbrance certificate should be obtained and verified. As far as leasehold properties are concerned the lease should be inspected where leasehold property has been sublet the counterpart of the tenant's agreement should be examined.

7. Plant and machinery

The existence of his asset should be verified by actual inspection. The auditor should call for the plant register and a schedule of plant and machinery certified by the registered engineer. This item should be valued on the basis of the value it should appear at original cost less depreciation written off to the date.

8. Loose tools

The auditor should examine the schedule of loose tools certified by a responsible officer. He should also examine the valuation sheet and see at it is properly certified.

9. Motor vehicles

They should be verified by actual inspection with reference to the vehicles registration or vehicles account. The auditor should examine the registration book for each vehicle. The auditor should also verity the adequacy for depreciation provide for:

10. Furniture fittings and fixtures

These assets should be verified by actual inspection with reference to the register concerned.

11. Patents

The inspector of the patents themselves should verify this asset. The certificate of grant of patents obtained from the authority should be examined. While examining the certificate the auditor should verify the last renewal certificate so as to know the currency of patents.

12. Copyright

The auditor should examine copyright in accordance with the copyright Act 1957 He should also verify the evidences/ certificates received in this connection.

13. Goodwill

It is a peculiar asset, it is by nature an intangible asset, it does not suffer from wear and tear and does not become obsolete, not consumed in the course of the business operations while verifying these assets it is enough the auditor ascertains that the value shown or the value decided does not exceed cost price.

Verification of Liabilities

The following are the various liabilities that are to be verified by the auditor in cooperatives.

1. Share capital

It should be verified with reference to the corresponding entries in the admission book.

2. Deposits

The amounts of deposits should be verified with reference to the confirmation cards received from the deposit holders as on the date of the balance sheet.

3. Creditors

The amount due to suppliers of goods on credit should be verified with statements of accounts received from them.

4. Loans from banks

The amount due to the financing Bank in respect of principal and amount of interest should be verified with the reconciliation statement received from the bank.

Valuation of Assets and Liabilities

The Valuation of assets is an important matter in the preparation of the final account. The correctness of Profit and Loss Account and Balance sheet mainly depends on the proper valuation of assets and liabilities. The valuation of Liabilities is an easy matter. As a rule it is possible to ascertain the amounts of liabilities exactly except in the case of contingent liabilities. But, the difficulty is with the valuation of assets. It is easy to find out the existence of assets but difficult to value them correctly.

In practice, assets are valued according to certain conventional principles. Two bases are adopted in this respect. Certain assets are valued on the basis of market value or realizable value. Some are valued on the basis of their use value to the business as going concern. There is also another basis namely replacement value, which is the amount that would be required to purchase the similar new asset when the existing one becomes useless.

Auditors Duty

As regards the duty of an auditor in connection with the valuation of assets, he should examine the correctness of the valuation. He should note the purpose for which the asset is acquired and study the method adopted for valuation. He is remained to ascertain that the valuation mode appears to be fair and reasonable according to the accepted principles.

Self-learning Activity

Try to answer the following questions on your own:

1. How do you verify the following assets? (*a*) cash on hand; (*b*) investments; (*c*) debenture
2. How do you verify the liabilities? Specify the liabilities.
3. What do you mean by valuation of assets and liabilities?
4. What is the duty of an auditor as regards valuation of assets and liabilities?

Summary

- The auditors should value the assets and liabilities of a cooperative society as per the methods prescribed in the cooperative law and by-law of the cooperative.

22 Financial Statement Audit

Audit of Final Accounts

The examination of the final account and the Balance Sheet is the final phase of audit work. Final account is prepared at the end of every trading period in order to assess the result of the transactions for the period. Along with it, the Balance Sheet as on the last date of the period is complied. Balance Sheet is the apex of the structure of account keeping. It is a mountaintop from where we can see the full picture of the business at a glance. It is prepared in such a form and manner as to give a clear idea about the financial position of the business on the date. It is to this statement of affairs that an Auditor's report or certificate refers. Hence the examination of the Balance Sheet and the final account relating thereto is all the more important from the point of view of an effect audit.

The nature and form of the final account and the Balance Sheet varies according to the nature and the type of the business. From this point of view, business undertakings may be grouped under two categories, viz,:

(*a*) Trading concerns; and

(*b*) Non-trading concerns.

In the case of trading concerns, the final account constitutes the Profit and Loss account. It is usually divided into two sections:

1. The Profit and Loss account; and
2. The Profit and Loss Appropriation Account.

The first section, viz., the Trading Account shows the gross profit. The second section shows the net profit or loss and the third shows the manner in which the net profit or loss and the third show the manner in which the net profit has been appropriated. As regards the non-trading concerns, such as charities, clubs, etc., the final account is termed "the Income and Expenditure Account." The balance of this account represents the excess of income over expenditure, or vice versa.

In the case of cooperatives, forms of final account and the Balance Sheet are prescribed by the Department of Cooperation. The auditor should see that the position disclosed by the accounts reflects a clear and true state of affairs. He should also note that only items of a like nature are grouped together. There should be "sufficient subdivisions to make the accounts clear and intelligible." And there should not be any suppression of material facts.

It must be remembered that the final account is merely a summary of all the transactions for a period. It is constructed out of multifarious details. It discloses the combined effect of all such details. If the foundation (i.e., the entries in the various books of accounts) upon which the structure of the final accounts is laid is incorrect and false, the final account would also reflect an untrue position. Therefore, the correctness and truth of the final account depends on the accuracy of various records. As such, (the auditor should go behind the books, examine the entries to their source, ascertain the accuracy, and satisfy himself that the final account is a correct summary reflecting the actual state of affairs.) It should be a plain mirror, but not a concave or convex.

Trading Account (Or) Manufacturing and Trading Account

The Trading Account is relating to the trading activities (i.e., buying and selling) of a concern. The object of this account is show the result of trading activities for a period. The result is to be assessed from the value of the goods sold and the account for their cost. The former is the net sale proceeds (i.e. sales less returns). The latter is calculated by adding to the original cost of goods, the amount of direct charges such as carriage inwards, customs duties, wages etc., adjustment being made for the opening and closing stocks. The difference between the amount of sale proceeds and the amount of the cost of the goods sold is the gross profit. This is transferred to the Profit and Loss Account. The following form is said to be preferable to the ordinary form:

TRADING ACCOUNT
for the period ending....

Dr.			Cr.		
Particulars	**Amount**		**Particulars**	**Amount**	
	$.	**$.**		**$.**	**$.**
To Cost of goods sold-			By Sales Gross proceeds	30,500	
(*a*) Opening stock	3,000				
(*b*) Purchases	25,000		Less Sales returns	1,500	
less Returns	2,000	23,000			
(*c*) Direct Expenses (carriage inward, Wages, etc.)	1,000				
		27,000			
Less Closing Stock	3,500	23,500			
To Profit and Loss A/C (Gross profit Carried over)		5,500	...		
	$. 29,000		$. 29,000		

The one distinctive advantage of this form over the ordinary one is that it shows the cost of the goods sold clearly and this figure can be calculated as a rate per cent of the sales and of the gross profit as well.

Rules of Principles

What are the rules governing the preparation of the Trading Account? Certain rules are adopted in preparing Trading Account as a matter of convention and uniformity. They may be summed up as follows:

1. Direct expenses incurred in connection with the purchase of goods are added to the cost of the goods; but such expenses as cartage outward relating to sales are not taken into the Trading Account.
2. Only the amounts of purchase and sales of goods in which the trading is carried on are included in the Trading Account.
3. The profits, if any, on the sale of an asset like furniture, etc., should not be treated as a trading profit.
4. For the purchase of preparation of the Trading Account for a period, the unsold stock of goods on hand as on the last date of that period is valued. The stock-in-trade is valued at cost or market price whichever is lower.

The Profit and Loss Account

The Profit and Loss Account is a consolidated summary of nominal accounts including the gross profit or loss transferred from the Trading Account. This account shows the net result of all transactions including the trading transactions for a particular period. The balance of the Trading Account is brought over to the Profit and Loss Account. It is, then, credited with all items of income such as discount, interest on investments, commission, etc., and debited with all items of expenses and losses like salaries, rent, etc. The expenses may be grouped under the headings of Selling and Distribution, Management, Financial Charges, and Maintenance and Depreciation. The amount of individual items under each head should be recorded in the inner column and the total of each head extended in the outer column. This would improve the form of the Profit and Loss Account from practical point of view.

PROFIT AND LOSS ACCOUNT

for the year ended....

Dr.			Cr.		
Particulars	Amount		Particulars	Amount	
	$	$		$.	$.
To Selling and			By Trading Account		
Distribution Expenses-			(gross profit b/f)		
Store rent	...		By Miscellaneous		
Packing charges	...		Income		
Advertising	...		Cash discount	...	
Cartage outward	...		Income from		
bad debts, etc.	...		investments		
	...	...	Commission, etc.	...	
To Management Expenses					
Salaries	...				
Office rent	...				
Printing & Stationery	...				
Postage	...				
Audit Fees, etc.	...				
	...	...			
To Financial Charges-					
Cash discount	...				
Interest on capital	...				
Interest on loans etc.	...				
To Maintenance and Depreciation-					
Repairs and renewals	...				
Depreciation on assets	...				
			...	...	
To Profit and Loss Appropriation Account-					
(Net profit carried over)	...	...			
	$.	...		$.	...

It is essential that this Account should be so drawn up as to disclose full information as a glance. It should also enable an easy comparison to be made for the various expenses and the sources of incomes with similar items of the previous years. The grouping of expenses under different heads facilitates such comparison. The calculation of percentage of each group of expenses to the turnover or to the total expenditure affords valuable information. And if the accounts are kept in a uniform basis, a comparison of these percentage with those of previous periods will provide information of lasting importance.

The Auditor should see that the Profit and Loss Account represents a true view of the normal earnings of the business during the period under review. Abnormal items, if any, should be shown separately in Account. For instance, a transfer to the Profit and Loss Account from a Reserve credited in the past years a non-recurring item. The fact of the transfer should be made clear so that false view may not be given of the earnings of the current period.

The Auditor should see that the following points are strictly observed in the preparation of the Profit and Loss Account:

1. Only such items of incomes and expenses as properly belonging to the business should be included in the Account.
2. The items included should be relating to the period under review, outstandings being brought into the Account.
3. There should be proper grouping and classification of items so as to present a clear picture of the current earnings.
4. Each item of income or expense should be shown under an appropriate head.
5. The whole Account should be prepared upon a consistant and uniform basis from year to year so as to facilitate useful comparison.

The Programme for a Final Accounts Audit

After vouching of all transaction and checking of postings to ledgers, final account is audited. The following are the principal items to be included in a programme for such an audit.

1. Compare the items appearing in the Trading and Profit and Loss Account with the Trial Balance/Statement of Receipts and Payments and the schedule of adjustment items.
2. Compare each item in the Trading and Profit and Loss Account with the corresponding item for previous year and go into the causes for wider variations.
3. Examine whether any increases or decreases in wages, materials consumed and overhead charges are proportionate to the increases or decrease in turnover.
4. Compare the rate of gross profit with that of previous year and ascertain the reasons for any material change.
5. Examine the reasons for similar variation, if any, in the net profit.
6. Compare the ratio of value of stock of turnover with that of previous year and enquire into any material variation.

The Profit and Loss Appropriate Account

This account is the last section of the Profit and Loss Account. This is of much use in companies and corporations. The Profit and Loss Appropriation Account shows the manner in which the profit is distributed among various items. The Account includes the balance of Profits and Loss Account carried forward from the previous year and the amount of the new profit or loss for the current year. All appropriations such as income tax, transfers to general reserve, dividends etc., are made in the Appropriation Account. The final balance is carried forward and shown in the Balance Sheet. The auditor should verify this account with reference to the previous year's Audit Report and minutes of the general meeting in which profit distribution was resolved. He should see whether profits have been distributed according to the Act, Rules and Bye-laws.

Audit of Balance Sheet

To recall you, let us define balance sheet and related aspects on balance sheet. The Balance Sheet is an all-important statement, but easy to be misunderstood. It is not an account like the Profit and Loss Account. But it is simply a 'sheet' of balances. It shows in a classified form, all the balances remaining in the books, after the nominal accounts have been closed. (It is generally thought that the Balance Sheet is a statement of Liabilities and Assets. But this definition is incomplete. Of course, it includes all the assets and liabilities of the business as on the date. However, it also in cludes, in many cases, items which are neither "liabilities" nor "assets" in the true sense of the words For example, the credit balance of Profit and Loss Account, Reserve Funds, amount received on forfeited shares, etc, are included on the left-hand side of the Balance Sheet. They are not really liabilities Again the debit balance of Profit and Loss Account, preliminary expenses, etc, appear on the right-hand side of the Balance Sheet, but they cannot be termed 'assets'.

A balance sheet has been defined as a classified summary of all the balances appearing in a set of books, after all the nominal accounts have been closed by transfer to the final account, the balance of which being also included in the sheet. All items of assets and other debit balances left open are shown on the right-hand side and the liabilities and other credit balances left unclosed are set out on the left-hand side of the sheet. In short, a Balance Sheet is a statement of affairs prepared with a view to ascertaining the exact financial position of the business on a particular date.

Because of these considerations, eminent authors like De Paula are of the view that a Balance Sheet should not have the sides headed 'Liabilities' and 'Assets'. The signs 'Dr.' and 'Cr.' should nor appear on it, since it is not a Ledger Account, nor should the terms 'To' and 'By' be used. A Balance Sheet should, therefore, have no headings, no signs and no terms; it should remain simply a plain statement of balances.

No hard and fast rule can be laid down as regards the form of a Balance Sheet. The balances are properly grouped and arranged in some logical order. Two methods of arrangements are employed. In the first, the assets are shown in the reverse order of their realisability. That is, Fixed Assets are shown first. Floating Assets next and Liquid Assets like cash in the last. On the other side, the liabilities are shown in the reverse order of repayment. Capital is shown first, reserves next and credit balance of the Profit and Loss Account last.

The second method is to marshall the assets and liabilities in exactly the reverse order. The assets are arranged in the order of liquidity. Liquid Assets are shown first and are followed by Floating Assets, Fixed Assets and Goodwill. On the other side, the liabilities are shown in the order in which they are payable. Current Liabilities like outstanding Expenses, Bills Payable, Sundry Creditors are shown first, while Capital is shown last.

The first method now seems to be followed by almost all concerns except banks and financial houses. The banks use a composite arrangement. They prefer to show the Liquid and the Floating Assets first and follow them up with the fixed Assets. The left hand side follows the first method and shows the Capital first. In the case of joint-stock companies and banks, the prescribed forms of Balance Sheet under the Indian Companies Act and the Banking Companies' Act respectively should be rigidly observed.

In America, it is customary to show the assets and other debit balances on the left-hand side and the capital and liabilities on the right-hand side. In co-operative concerns, the forms prescribed by the Registrar for respective societies should be adopted. Whatever may be the form, the Balance Sheet should be such as to reflect the true position of the business and the concerned persons should easily understand it.

The purpose of a Balance Sheet: "The Balance Sheet is the culmination of the system of book-keeping". The object with which a Balance Sheet is prepared is three-fold:

(i) to ascertain the exact financial position of the business on a date;

(ii) to see whether the capital is kept intact or not; and

(iii) to study the manner in which such capital stands invested.

The correctness of the financial position as disclosed by the Balance Sheet depends on the accuracy with which the assets and liabilities are valued. But it is impossible to fix such values with absolute precision. The difficultly involved in making a precise valuation, therefore, sets out a limitation to the precision of a Balance Sheet.

In no way an absolute exactitude and certainty can be achieved in the periodical accounts of a business. No body can claim for an audited Balance Sheet absolute exactitude There are limitations of valuation, limitations of audit in general and limitations of many hypothetical matters. A Balance Sheet, whatever be the thoroughness with which it is prepared, can only show the fairest possible estimate of the position of affairs, arrived at in accordance with accepted conventional rules and principles as regards valuation and other matters.

The Programme for a Balance Sheet Audit

A Balance Sheet Audit should cover the following main items:

1. Compare each item of Balance Sheet with the corresponding figures for the previous period and go into material changes.

2. Consider the ratio of sundry debtors to turnover with that of the previous year and enquire into any material change in the ratio.
3. Examine the adequacy of provisions made for bad and doubtful debts.
4. Examine the amount of sundry creditors in relation to the turnover, stock-in-trade and the period of credit normally taken.
5. Compare the list of outstanding assets and liabilities with that of the previous year and ascertain the reasons for material changes, if any.
6. Examine the minute books for any resolutions affecting the accounts.
7. Scrutinize the values of assets.
8. Examine the adequacy of provisions made for depreciation.
9. Find out the amounts of contingent liabilities.
10. Verify assets and liabilities shown in the Balance Sheet.
11. Examine the form of the Balance Sheet.

Misappropriations and Frauds

Misappropriation of Cash

All human beings are not perfectly honest. Prompted by selfish motives, some persons commit misappropriations and frauds. Cooperatives are no exception to this general trend. In some cases their office bearers and employees resort to misaproriation or defalcation of cash or goods and misuse the properties of the cooperatives for their personal purposes.

Cash in generally beset with temptations. It is misappropriated either by omitting or under-recording of cash receipts or by including fictitious payments.

Cash Receipts: Some of the methods adopted for misappropriating cash received are:

1. In smaller societies composed of illiterate persons as members, the scope for misappropriation of cash is greater. Members who remit share capital or repay loans may not insist on receipts for the amounts paid by them. In such cases the dishonest president or cashier, as the case may be, easily misappropriates cash, by omitting to record cash received from such parties. No receipt is prepared for amounts received and no entries are made in the Day Book. Only a thorough verification of share capital and loans could reveal such misappropriations.
2. Another method adopted for misappropriation cash is noting the correct amount received in the original or foil issued to the party and a lower amount in the counterfoil of duplicate. The amount shown in the counterfoil or duplicate alone is brought into the account and the balance is misappropriated. This kind of fraud can be detected if the auditor asks the members to produce the original receipts for verification.
3. One full leaf of the Receipt book, both foil and counterfoil, generally the last one, may be removed and used for granting receipts to two different persons. The entire amount may be misappropriated. The auditor should see if all the unused receipts are in fact and the serial numbers are continuous. He should collect confirmation of accounts by the parties and compare them with book balances to discover such frauds.
4. The Secretary/Cashier may use separate receipt book without the knowledge of other connected with the society. He may issue receipts for moneys received from members and misappropriate them. This kind of fraud can be detected only when members dispute the balances shown against their names and produce the receipts issued to them.
5. Temporary receipts in plain paper may be issued for amounts received and the amounts so received may be

misappropriated. In some cases entries for amounts received may be made directly in the passbook, without issue of any receipts. These kinds of frauds may be detected only by a personal verification of the members, and their pass books with the ledger.

6. Misappropriation of cash may be resorted by manipulating totals, balances and carry forwards. This kind of fraud will be discovered if totals, balances, etc. carefully checked.

7. There are also the possibilities of altering the figures in the counterfoil of receipts after the originals are issued to the parties. The auditor should be careful if there are scorings or alterations, and call for the original receipts from the parties and locate the extent of defalcations made.

Payments: Misappropriation of cash by falsification of vouchers may also be done. Some of the methods used for this purpose are:

1. Forged vouchers for refund of share capital to members who have expired or left the place may be created and the corresponding amounts of cash may be misappropriated.

   A careful comparison of the signatures in vouchers with the specimen signatures of the members concerned will reveal such frauds.

2. Benami loans (in other's name) are crated in the records and the loan amounts are misappropriated. Only a very careful verification of loans with the persons in whose names the loans appear in the books will reveal this kind of fraud.

3. The Secretary may misappropriate amount of renewed fixed deposits by showing them in accounts as refunded on the basis of forged vouchers. He may succeed in concealing such misappropriation for some time by paying

interest on such deposits out of his own funds. When depositors who claim refund complaint, the cat will be out of the bag. A careful scrutiny of the signatures in the refund vouchers with the original signatures of the depositors will reveal these frauds.

4. False travelling allowances bills may be prepared and recorded in the accounts.

   A careful scrutiny of such vouchers and an enquiry into the purposes for which journeys purported to have been made will help discovering such frauds.

Temporary Misappropriation of Cash

Where heavy cash balance is maintained regularly, a part of the balance may be taken for private use and may be made good later. This kind of fraud can be discovered by surprise verification of cash balance. The best way to prevent such temporary misappropriations is to see that cash balances in excess of bare minimum requirement are not maintained.

In rural cooperatives, the presidents may keep the cash balance in their houses. Generally they mix up societies' cash with their private cash. Such mixing may lead to temporary misappropriation even without their knowledge.

It is necessary to insist that the cash balance of the society is kept in a separate bag.

Defalcation of Goods

In the case of societies like consumers' cooperative stores, marketing cooperative, house construction societies etc. stock of materials and goods may be misappropriated by falsification of accounts.

Some of the methods of such defalcation of goods are:

1. Books may show dispose of it privately and misappropriate the money. A careful verification of each item of stock with reference to the stock register will reveal such frauds.

2. The Salesmen of a consumer cooperative stores may resort to under-measurement or under-weighment and defalcate the excess stock. A surprise verification of packages of the customers coming out of the stores with the bills will reveal such under-measurement or under-weighment.

3. Cooperative urban banks usually provide safe-custody facilities and issue loans against pledge of jewels. In these cases the manager in charge of duplicate keys of safety lockers and vaults may collide with the appraiser and may replace valuables and tamper with jewels and share the illegal gain. Complaints from customers and borrowers may reveal such frauds.

4. The manager and his assistants of a branch of a consumers' cooperative stores dealing in controlled and rationed articles may create false sales bills and sell the corresponding goods in black market at higher prices. Surprise verification of stocks and enquires with cardholders to whom sales have been purported to have been made will bring out such frauds.

Whenever an auditor suspects or discovers a fraud, he should go deep into the matter and send a special confidential report to the district auditor or the Deputy Registrar concerned, who will make further investigation and arrange for booking criminal cases against the culprits.

Self-learning Activity

Try to answer the following questions on your own:

1. What is the duty of an auditor as regards profit and loss account?
2. What is the programme for a balance sheet audit?
3. What is misappropriation of cash?
4. What are the methods used for misappropriation of payments?
5. Specify some of the methods of defalcation of goods.

Summary

- Based on the programme for final accounts audit and balance sheet audit the auditor should exercise his duty regarding financial statement audit. He should verify necessary evidences and disclose the misappropriation and frauds.

23 Cooperative Audit Practices in Ethiopia

Departmental set up of Cooperative Audit

It remains to consider by whom final/financial audit may be carried out. In some cases the law merely lays down that a properly qualified professional accountant other than one of their own employees shall audit cooperatives. In other cases audit is entrusted to a central cooperative body. Finally, in some cases the law provides that the auditor shall be a government official or that government appointed auditors must be employed unless and until the cooperatives can satisfy the government that they have been able to set up an auditing system of their own employing professional accountants of the necessary status and qualifications. The result is that there are three systems with a certain amount of overlap between them.

Private Agencies: One method is for the cooperatives to employ a private professional auditor who may specialize in cooperative work but probably also audits other business. In some countries, where a government department regularly audits the smaller primary cooperatives, the larger federal organizations are advised to employ outside professional auditors.

Central Cooperative Bodies: The second system is for auditing to be placed in the hands of a central cooperative body. A special auditing union does not always carry out central cooperative auditing. It may be the function of a general cooperative union, a national cooperative bank or wholesale society.

Government Departments: The third method is audit by a government department. The justification for giving the department ultimate responsibility for audit lies in the fact that the cooperative movement has usually been introduced and is still in many ways supported by the government, which must be regularly informed of its progress and shortcomings.

Departmental set up of Cooperative Audit in Ethiopia

The administrative set up of cooperative audit department in Ethiopia is discussed hereunder. The Federal Cooperative Agency has got the Audit wing under the control of the appropriate authority as per the Cooperative Proclamation. Under the federal agency there are fourteen regional cooperative promotion bureaus in the country. The regional bureaus are having audit wing in order to control over the zonal level audit wing, which is responsible for conducting audit in the cooperative societies of various types. The zonal bureau is the responsible body for the audit process/work at the zonal levels. There is an audit and inspection team under the control of the zonal Cooperative Promotion Officer. It comprises of one team leader, auditors, audit assistants, inspectors and inspector assistants. The auditors and inspectors are responsible for conducting audit in all cooperative societies under the control of zonal head. The following chart depicts the picture of cooperative audit team at zonal level.

Powers, Duties and Responsibilities of Cooperative Auditor

Powers of Cooperative Auditor

1. He shall at all times, have access to all the books of accounts, documents, papers, securities, cash and other properties belonging to or in the custody of the society.

Zonal level Cooperative Audit and Inspection Team

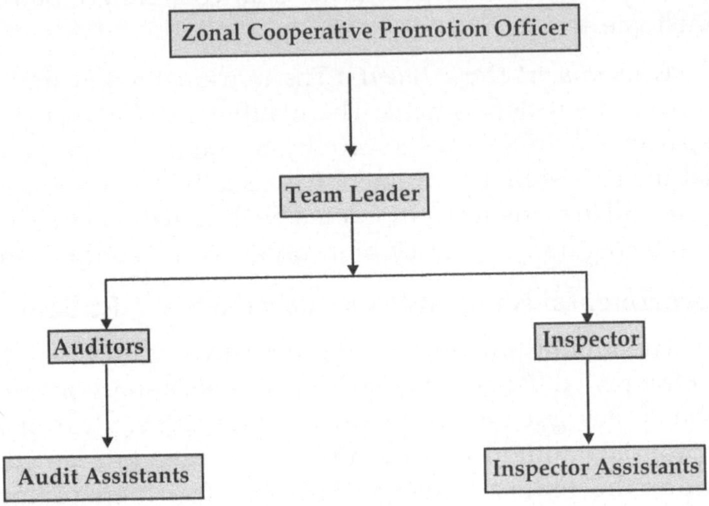

Fig. 23.1

2. The auditor can issue summon for immediate production of books and cash serve it on the person responsible to produce the same, the auditor has power to summon and enforce the attendance of any person and examine him to oath and to issue commission for examination of witness.
3. He shall have the power to receive required information regard to the transactions and working of the society from every officer, employee, and member, past or present, of the society.
4. If the auditor has reason to believe that any book or other property of the society is likely to be tempered with, he shall have the power to seize them.
5. The auditor shall have the right to receive all notices and communication relating to the annual general meeting and to attend such meeting where his report is being discussed.

Duties and Responsibilities

Audit shall include examination or verification as the duties of cooperative auditor of the following items:

1. Overdue debts, if any;
2. Cash balance and securities, and valuation of assets and liabilities;
3. Whether loans and advances and debts of the society made are properly secured and in the best interests of the society and its members;
4. Whether transactions recorded in the books of accounts are not prejudicial to the interests of the society;
5. Whether loans and advances have been shown as deposits;
6. Whether personal expenses have been charged to revenue account;
7. Whether any expenditure is against the objects of the society;
8. Whether financial assistance given by government or any other agencies has been utilize for the purpose for which it was sanctioned;
9. Whether the society is properly carrying out its objects and obligations towards the members;
10. Drawing up of audit programme for the societies and getting the approval from the District (Woreda) Audit officer;
11. The auditor shall submit an audit memorandum duly signed by him on the accounts and profit and loss account, and balance sheet examined by him and shall state whether in his opinion and to the best of his information and according to the explanation given to him by the society, present the true and fair view of the financial transactions of the society;

12. A separate register should be maintained by the auditor to note the progress of audit, which is to be scrutinized and to make remarks by the superiors;
13. Copies of the tour programme and diaries should be submitted to the superiors;
14. With prior permission from the Registrar the auditor may impound the books or documents and receipts thereof to the society if during the course of audit of any society, the auditor is satisfied that some books of accounts of other documents contain any incriminatory evidence against past or present officer, employee of the society; and
15. Auditor engaged in the audit process of cooperative societies must know ratio analysis system in audit.

Legal Aspects of Cooperative Audit

Ethiopian Cooperative Proclamation and Audit

Part four of the Cooperative Proclamation No.147/1998 deals with the Audit and Inspection of cooperative societies in Ethiopia. Article 36, 37, 38 and 39 are dealing with the audit, inspection, keeping audit and inspection results and actions to be taken for losses of property or fund of the society.

Article 36. Audit

1. The appropriate authority shall audit or causes to be audited by a person assigned by it, the accounts of any society at least once in a year.
2. The audit conducted pursuant to Sub-Article (1) of this Article shall include the examination and verification of overdue debts, if any, cash balance, securities and assets, and liabilities.
3. The audit report shall be submitted to the general assembly.

Article 37. Inspection

1. The appropriate authority may, make cause to be made by such person to be assigned by it an inspection to the organization, work execution, documents and financial condition of a society.
2. Without prejudice to Sub-Article (1) of this Article inspection may be made when:
   (*a*) a majority of the members of the executive committee request.
   (*b*) not less than one-third of the total number of members of the society request.

Article 38. Keeping Audit and Inspection Results

Audit and Inspection result conducted pursuant to Article 36 and 37 of this Proclamation shall be kept in the office of the authority and the society, open and easily accessible to everyone.

Article 39. Actions to be taken for Losses of Property or Fund of the Society

1. The auditor or inspector shall make report to the management committee or the general assembly or the appropriate authority, as the case may be, where the person who is or was entrusted with the management of the society or who is or has been an officer or an employee of the society, and who in the course of an audit or inspection has been found to have committed the following acts:
   (*a*) had made any payment contrary to this Proclamation, the regulations or the by-laws;
   (*b*) has caused any damages to the assets of the society by breach of trust or willfully or negligently;
   (*c*) has misappropriated the properties of the society.

2. The appropriate authority who received the report pursuant to Sub-Article 1 of this Article shall give the person concerned an opportunity to present his defense within fifteen days.
3. After fulfillment of the above mentioned conditions, the appropriate authority shall ask the person who has been found responsible for misappropriation of the fund or property of the society to return or pay same with interest including compensation and damages. Where the person concerned is not willing to do so, the authority shall take the appropriate legal measure.

Audit Classification of Cooperatives in Ethiopia

After completion of audit, that is after preparing the final accounts and balance sheet, by following the instructions issued by the Registrar of Cooperative Societies/appropriate authority/Zonal Cooperative Audit Officer, the auditor has to classify the society. Observing the capital structure, credit and financial stability, management and other service function of a society makes the classification. The credit and financial stability covers the extent of credit provided and the efforts made to recover the same. The management aspect covers the rectification of defects noted in the previous year audit reports, action taken against defaulters, holding meetings, maintenance of books and records/accounts of the society and how far the management can able to satisfy and fulfill the needs and interests of the members of the society. So, the audit classification of the society is aiming to test the financial position and stability and management and administrative efficiency of a cooperative society.

In Ethiopia, the audit classification is done under four broad categories by measuring the society in terms of the above-mentioned criteria, and the cooperative societies are classified into Green, Blue, Yellow and Red.

- *The Green colour* notifies that the cooperative society is running/functioning well in accordance with the norms and Cooperative Proclamation (These societies are sound enough in all aspects and follow the cooperative principles);

- *Blue* notifies that the cooperative society is functioning fairly by following the norms (These societies are also financially sound enough but they lack cooperative spirit);
- *Yellow* classification will be given as a warning signal to the cooperative society to function in accordance with the by-laws and cooperative proclamation and based on the norms (These societies face problems of extensive dependence even for working capital); and
- *Red* will be given to dormant cooperative societies for liquidation (These societies are either dormant or may become dormant soon).

The above are the audit classifications, which are being given by the auditors after completion of the audit process.

Audit Report and Audit Certificate

Preparation of audit report is a difficult task as compared to audit work. Though the auditor has completed his work honestly and with dedication but it will be in vein if the audit report is not return in correct manner. So, audit report should be written with great care and he should be careful enough in the followings as stated earlier in the second module:

1. The language of audit report should be explicit and defective.
2. In audit report answers to the given questions should be correct, complete and exhaustive.
3. Objections raised in previous audit should be scrutinized and it should be seen how for they are removed.
4. Complete details should be given for the proceedings which are to be done according to cooperative principles, the Cooperative Proclamation, bylaws and the departmental directions.

5. Details of errors found in books and registers of the society should be spelt out.
6. The mistakes and errors observed during audit work should be written at proper place in the audit report.
7. The cash balance and the stock should be examined and their positions should be given in an explicit manner.
8. All vouchers of the year other information report and the auditor should initiate audited errors and then it should be attached with the audit report.
9. If the society had received any aid then its utilization should be examined and verification should be made in the audit report.
10. Audit report should not only be critical but should also be suggestive hence suggestions should be given for the improvement in the performance of the society.

The Cooperative Auditor is required to state the following points:

1. Audit report must be specific and accurate, based on books of account and documents examined;
2. Major and minor lapses need to be mentioned in the report;
3. The auditor must record his observations, remarks, opinions, inferences, etc.
4. The audit report should invariable accompanied by the following list inaddition to balance sheet:

   Receipts and Payments statement, trading account, profit and loss account, list of members, list of defaulters, list of stocks and dead stocks, list of creditors/debtors related statements deemed to be necessary.

5. Particulars of all transactions which appear to be contrary to me provisions of the Act, Proclamation, Rules and by-laws of the society.

6. All sums which ought to have been but have not been brought into accounts by the society.
7. Any money or property belonging to the society which appear to be bad or doubtful debts/doubtful of recovery.
8. Any other matter specified by the Registrar in this behalf.
9. The auditor is required to provide information regarding share capital, borrowings, meetings, staff structure, etc., of the society.

Audit Certificate

After writing or preparing the audit report, the auditor will prepare an audit certificate in the prescribed proforma and after duly signed he has to submit the same to the appropriate authority for approval. The Zonal head will receive the certificate and the report, and send it to the federal agency for getting signed. After that a copy of the audit certificate will be sent to the society concerned to keep it in the file. The audit report is copy also be kept in the society concerned for future reference and record.

Self-learning Activity

Try to answer the following questions on your own:

1. Discuss about the departmental set up of cooperative audit in Ethiopia?
2. What are the powers of a cooperative auditor?
3. Which Article of Cooperative Proclamation deals with audit of cooperative societies? Write the provisions made in the Article.
4. What are the Actions to be taken for Losses of Property or Fund of the Society?
5. Describe the audit classifications of cooperatives in Ethiopia?
6. What is the procedure regarding audit certificate?

Summary

- At the federal agency there is a wing for audit; at the regional bureaus audit and inspection wing is established. The zonal office has audit and inspection wing to audit and inspect the cooperatives at the grassroot level. Green, Blue, Yellow and Red colours are given as audit classification for cooperatives in Ethiopia.
- The audit report is to be prepared and audit certificate is also be prepared by the auditor and it should be sent for approval of appropriate authority as per the articles of the Cooperative Proclamation.

References

Krishnaswami.O.R. (1971), "Principles of Cooperative Audit", Karthikeya Publishing House, Chennai, India.

Manickavasagam.P., (1992), "A Treatise on Cooperative Account Keeping", Rainbow Publications.

Shekhar and Shekhar.,(2003), 'Auditing', Vikas Publishing House Pvt. Ltd.

Ravinder Kumar and Virender Sharma,(2001), "Fundamentals of Practical Auditing", PHI.

Alvin A Arens and James K Loebbecke, "Auditing — An Integrated Approach" (4th Edn), Prentice Hall International.

Further Readings

Abbott, L. J., S. Parker and G. F. Peters. 2010. Serving two masters: The Association Between Audit Committee Internal Audit Oversight and Internal Audit Activities. *Accounting Horizons* (March): 1-24.

Abdel-Khalik, A.R., D. Snowball and J. H. Wragge. 1983. The Effects of Certain Internal Audit Variables on the Planning of External Audit Programmes. *The Accounting Review* (April): 215-227. (JSTOR link).

AICPA. 1975. *Statement on Auditing Standards No. 5: The Meaning of "Present Fairly in Conformity with Generally Accepted Accounting Principles" in the Independent Auditor's Report*. AICPA.

AICPA. 2008. *Audit Sampling Audit Guide*. AICPA.

Almer, E.D., J.L. Higgs and K. L. Hooks. 2005. A Theoretical Framework of the Relationship Between Public Accounting Firms and Their Auditors. *Behavioural Research in Accounting* (17): 1-22.

Apostolou, N. and D. L. Grumbley. 2008. Auditors' Responsibilities with Respect to Fraud: A Possible Shift? *The CPA Journal* (February): 32-37.

Arens, A. A., M.S. Elder and R.J. Beasley. 2005. *Auditing and Assurance Services (10th Edition) (Charles T Horngren Series in Accounting)*. Prentice Hall.

Ashton, A.H. 1991. Experience and Error Frequency Knowledge as Potential Determinants of Audit Expertise. *The Accounting Review* (April): 218-239. (JSTOR link). (Part of a Forum on Cognitive Research in Auditing).

Ashton, R.H. 1974. An Experimental Study of Internal Control Judgements. *Journal of Accounting Research* (Spring): 143-157. (JSTOR link).

Ashton, R.H. and A.M. Cianci. 1998. Contributions of the "Research Opportunities in Auditing" Programme: An Empirical Assessment. *Accounting Horizons* (June): 120-138.

Bailey, A.D. Jr., W.J. Boe and T. Schnack. 1974. The Audit Staff Assignment Problem: A Comment. *The Accounting Review* (July): 572-574. (JSTOR link).

Bailey, G.D. 1950. Current Auditing Problems. *The Accounting Review* (April): 125-132. (JSTOR link).

Bailey, K.E. III, J.H. Bylinski and M.D. Shields. 1983. Effects of Audit Report Wording Changes on the Perceived Message. *Journal of Accounting Research* (Autumn): 355-370. (JSTOR link).

Bailey, W. T. 1982. An Appraisal of Research Designs used to Investigate the Information Content of Audit Reports. *The Accounting Review* (January): 141-146. (JSTOR link).

Balachandran, B.V. and R.T.S. Ramakrishnan. 1987. A Theory of Audit Partnerships: Audit Firm Size and Fees. *Journal of Accounting Research* (Spring): 111-126. (JSTOR link).

Barkman, A. 1977. Within-item Variation: A Stochastic Approach to Audit Uncertainty. *The Accounting Review* (April): 450-464. (JSTOR link).

Barkman, A.I. 1978. Within-item Variation: A Stochastic Approach to Audit Uncertainty — A Reply. *The Accounting Review* (October): 993-996. (JSTOR link).

Bell, W.H. 1919. Audit Working Papers. *Journal of Accountancy* (August): 104-112.

Bharadwaj, A., V. Karan, R.K. Mahapatra, U.S. Murthy and A.S. Vinze. 1994. APX: An Integrated Knowledge-based System to Support Audit Planning. *International Journal of Intelligent Systems in Accounting, Finance, and Management* 3(3): 149-164.

Bonner, S.E. and B.L. Lewis. 1990. Determinants of Auditor Expertise. *Journal of Accounting Research* (Studies on Judgement in Accounting and Auditing): 1-20. (JSTOR link).

Borthick, A.F. and P.L. Bowen. 2008. Auditing System Development: Constructing the Meaning of "Systematic and Rational" in the Context of Legacy Code Migration. *Journal of Information Systems* (Spring): 47-62.

Brighton, G. D. 1954. Aid to Management Beyond the Audit. *The Accounting Review* (October): 584-590. (JSTOR link).

Buist, G. B. 1922. Purposes and Limitations of a Balance Sheet Audit. *Journal of Accountancy* (September): 182-189.

DeAngelo, L.E. 1981. Auditor Independence, 'Low Balling', and Disclosure Regulation. *Journal of Accounting and Economics* (August): 113-127.

Dunn, C.L. and G.J. Gerard. 2001. Auditor Efficiency and Effectiveness with Diagrammatic and Linguistic Conceptual Model Representations. *International Journal of Accounting Information Systems* 2(4): 223-248.

Epaves, R.A., L.R. Paquette and M.A. Pearson. 1976. A Flow Chart Conceptualization of Auditors' Reports on Financial Statements. *The Accounting Review* (October): 913-916. (JSTOR link).

Fisher, K. 2009. *How to Smell a Rat: The Five Signs of Financial Fraud*. John Wiley & Sons.

Graham, L. and W.F. Messier Jr. 2006. Audit Risk and Materiality in Conducting an Audit. *Journal of Accountancy* (May): 116-123.

Grimlund, R.A. 1982. An Integration of Internal Control System and Account Balance Evidence. *Journal of Accounting Research* (Part I, Autumn): 316-342. (JSTOR link).

Hay, R.D. 1975. Social Auditing: An Experimental Approach. *The Academy of Management Journal* 18(4): 871-877. (JSTOR link).

Lafrentz, F.W. 1906. Economic Aspects of Accounting and Auditing. *Journal of Accountancy* (April): 479-486.

Lafrentz, F.W. 1924. Defalcations. *Journal of Accountancy* (April): 254-261.

Lin, Z., Q.Tang and Z.J. Xiao. 2003. An Experimental Study of Users' Responses to Qualified Audit Reports in China. *Journal of International Accounting, Auditing & Taxation* 12(1): 1-22.

Masonson, L.N. 1989. The Cash Management Audit. *Management Accounting* (March): 40-43.

McCray, J.H. 1973. Ratio and Difference Estimation in Auditing. *Management Accounting* (December): 45-48.

McCray, J.H. 1984. A Quasi-Bayesian Audit Risk Model for Dollar Unit Sampling. *The Accounting Review* (January): 35-51. (JSTOR link).

McCray, J. H. 1984. A Quasi-Bayesian Audit Risk Model for Dollar Unit Sampling: A Reply. *The Accounting Review* (July): 526-527. (JSTOR link).

McDaniel, L.S. 1990. The Effects of Time Pressure and Audit Programme Structure on Audit Performance. *Journal of Accounting Research* (Autumn): 267-285. (JSTOR link).

McDaniel, L.S. and W.R. Kinney, Jr. 1995. Expectation-formation Guidance in the Auditor's Review of Interim Financial Information. *Journal of Accounting Research* (Spring): 59-76. (JSTOR link).

McEnroe, J.E. 1993. An Analysis of Comment Integration Involving SAS 54. *Abacus* 29(2): 160-178.

McEnroe, J.E. 2002. An Analysis of Post-expectation Gap Voting Behaviour by the ASB. *Abacus* 38(3): 350-377.

McEnroe, J.E. and S.C. Martens. 2001. Auditors' and Investors' Perceptions of the 'Expectation Gap'. *Accounting Horizons* (December): 345-358.

McGladrey, I.B. 1947. Problems in Assuming Proper Responsibility. *The Accounting Review* (July): 273-280. (JSTOR link).

McGladrey, I. B. 1951. The Audit Report. *The Accounting Review* (April): 197-208. (JSTOR link).

McHugh, W.J. 1976. ERISA — A New Audit Headache for Management. *Management Accounting* (April): 21-28.

McKee, T. E. 2009. A Meta-learning Approach to Predicting Financial Statement Fraud. *Journal of Emerging Technologies in Accounting* (6): 5-26.

McKee, T.E. 2010. The 'Cry Wolf' Problem in Current Fraud Auditing Standards. *The CPA Journal* (January): 60-62.

Morse, E.H. Jr. 1973. Comments on Survey of Attitudes on Management Auditing. *The Accounting Review* (January): 120-122. (JSTOR link).

O'Malley, S. 1993. Legal Liability is having a Chilling Effect on the Auditor's Role. *Accounting Horizons* (June): 82-87.

Peak, G.W. 1940. Auditing Assessment Accuracy. *The Accounting Review* (June): 238-241. (JSTOR link).

Penno, M. 1990. Auditing for Performance Evaluation. *The Accounting Review* (July): 520-536. (JSTOR link).

Quinn, L.R. 2002. Strengthening the Role of the Audit Committee. *Strategic Finance* (December): 42-47.

Radin, A.J. 2008. A Practical Approach to Finding Management Override. *The CPA Journal* (October): 6-9.

Raghunandan, K. and D.V. Rama. 2007. Determinants of Audit Committee Diligence. *Accounting Horizons* (September): 265-279.

Raghunandan, K., W.J. Read and D.V. Rama. 2001. Audit Committee Composition, 'Gray Directors', and Interaction with Internal Auditing. *Accounting Horizons* (June): 105-118.

Ramos, M. 2009. Risk-based Audit Best Practices. *Journal of Accountancy* (December): 32-38.

Richardson, A.P. 1919. Professional Ethics, Tax Return Makers, Efficiency, Value of Audited Statements, Auditor's Certificates. *Journal of Accountancy* (December): 451-457.

Ricchiute, D.N. 1992. Working-paper Order Effects and Auditors' Going-concern Decisions. *The Accounting Review* (January): 46-58. (JSTOR link).

Rittenberg, L.E. and B.J. Schwieger. 2003. *Auditing Concepts for a Changing Environment with IDEA Software, 4e*. South-Western Publishing.

Rogers, C. 2006. Continuous Monitoring of Business Controls: A Pilot Implementation of a Continuous Auditing System at Siemens: Discussant's Comments. *International Journal of Accounting Information Systems* 7(2): 167-169.

Scott, W.R. 1973. A Bayesian Approach to Asset Valuation and Audit Size. *Journal of Accounting Research* (Autumn): 304-330. (JSTOR link).

Sharman, P. 2003. External Audit Failure. *Cost Management* (September/October): 46-48.

Simini, P. 1963. The Scope Paragraph of the Audit Report Graphically Illustrated. *The Accounting Review* (January): 157-159. (JSTOR link).

Smith, C.D. 1955. Comments on Neter's "Problems in Experimenting with the Application of Statistical Techniques in Auditing". *The Accounting Review* (January): 70. (JSTOR link).

Smith, C.H. and R.A. Lanier. 1970. The Audit of Management: Report on a Field Study. *Management Accounting* (June):24-26, 46.

Sriram, R.S. 2008. Discussion of "X-Raying Segregation of Duties: Support to Illuminate an Enterprises' Immunity to Solo-fraud". *International Journal of Accounting Information Systems* 9(2): 94-96.

Tsui, J.S.L. and F.A. Gul. 1996. Auditors' Behaviour in an Audit Conflict Situation: A Research Note on the Role of Locus of Control and Ethical Reasoning. *Accounting, Organizations and Society* 21(1): 41-51.

Wells, J.T. 2009. Practical and Ethical Considerations in Fraud Examination. *The CPA Journal* (June): 56-58.

White, H.C. 1973. A Leadership Audit. *Management Accounting* (August): 39-41.

Wolf, R.G. 1976. Being Audited? Making it Easier is Upto You. *Management Accounting* (March): 27-28.

Wyatt, A.R. 1989. Accounting Standards and the Professional Auditor. *Accounting Horizons* (June): 96-102.

Yardley, J.A. 1989. Explaining the Conditional Nature of the Audit Risk Model. *Journal of Accounting Education* 7(1): 107-114.

Zhou, H. 2007. Auditing Standards, Increased Accounting Disclosure, and Information Asymmetry: Evidence from an Emerging Market. *Journal of Accounting and Public Policy* 26: 584-620.

Index

❑❑❑